Policy

Third Edition

CONCEPTS IN THE SOCIAL SCIENCES
Series editor: Frank Parkin

Published titles

Concepts in the Social Sciences

Policy

Third Edition

H. K. Colebatch

Open University Press

Open University Press
McGraw-Hill Education
McGraw-Hill House
Shoppenhangers Road
Maidenhead
Berkshire
England
SL6 2QL

email: enquiries@openup.co.uk
world wide web: www.openup.co.uk

and Two Penn Plaza, New York, NY 10121-2289, USA

First edition published 1997

A catalogue record of this book is available from the British Library

ISBN-10: 0335 2354 07 (pb)
ISBN-13: 978 0335 235409 (pb)

Library of Congress Cataloging-in-Publication Data
CIP data applied for

Typeset by YHT Ltd
Printed in the UK by Bell & Bain Ltd, Glasgow

Mixed Sources
Product group from well-managed
forests and other controlled sources
www.fsc.org   Cert no. TT-COC-002769
© 1996 Forest Stewardship Council
FSC

The McGraw·Hill Companies

To Peta
who knows all about policy
but doesn't have the time
to write it down

Contents

Preface

Policy is an idea which flows through all the ways in which we organize our life: it is used by a wide range of participants in public life – public officials, elected representatives, activists, experts, journalists and others – in their attempts to shape the way public life is organized. We encounter it inside organizations. For instance, we may find a homework policy in a secondary school, which clarifies the expectations of students, teachers and parents, or the question of when a hospital patient can go home may be governed by a discharge policy. We may find it being used across organizations. River pollution may be addressed by drawing up a catchment management policy that governs all the activities affecting the river. Employers, unions and technical colleges may together draw up an industry training policy. And we can see, too, that policy may be a way for activists outside the corridors of power to seek change. Activists were able to generate policy on issues such as global warming or equal employment opportunity.

But while policy seems to imply clear direction, the policy process seems to be characterized by conflict, resistance, uncertainty and ambiguity. Policy statements may be hard to interpret, they may be contradicted by other policy statements, and they may not have much to do with the way governing is conducted. Or there may be no statements, and policy may be something that has to be inferred from practice. This tension between clear purpose and ambiguous struggle pervades both the writing on policy and the experience of policy practice.

We have to remember that 'policy' is first of all a concept – that is, an idea that people use in making sense of the world – so we must understand it as a concept in the analysis of the process of government. How is it used? What does it make clear? How does it relate to other analytical constructs such as 'structure', 'process' or 'management'? We must remember, too, that 'policy' is not simply a label, but is part of the process which it describes. To speak of 'heritage policy', for instance, is not simply a neutral way of talking about something that is there, but a way of focusing attention on some things (such as the value of historic buildings) rather than others (such as the possibility of demolishing them and building a tower block of offices). So in examining the concept of policy, we need to take account of how it is used by practitioners as well as by academic observers.

This book is written for a range of readers, including both practitioners and observers. There are those who are interested in a particular field (such as the environment), and want to know what it means to have 'environmental policy' and how it is produced. There are students of the political process, who want to know how 'policy' (or 'public policy') relates to well-established analytical terms such as 'politics', 'rule-making' or 'decision'. And then there are those who are interested in the broader issue of the way in which we are governed, which seems to mean more than just 'what the government decides to do', and to be concerned with the way that diverse activities by different bodies are drawn together into stable and predictable patterns of action which (as often as not) come to be labelled 'policy'.

Acknowledgements

The analysis in this book has been shaped by more collegial discussion than I can possibly acknowledge. Bernard Schaffer first awakened my interest in policy, and I have benefited from years of friendship and discussion with John Ballard, Pieter Degeling, Peter Larmour and Mark Lyons. I have been greatly stimulated by colleagues and students at Kuring-gai College, the universities of Tasmania, New South Wales and Brunei Darussalaam, and Robert Gordon University, Aberdeen, and would particularly like to thank Chee Kim Loy, Sue Keen, Justin Greenwood, Darren Halpin, Shafruddin bin Hashim and Chris Walker for their collegial support and tolerance. I would like to thank Geoffrey Braithwaite and Barry Hindess at the Australian National University, and Dick Scott and Jim March at Stanford, for their hospitality and encouragement. I am particularly indebted to Randall Smith and his colleagues at the School for Policy Studies at the University of Bristol for their collegial support over the years. The Press's three readers provided a particularly constructive critique of the second edition, and I am grateful to Sally Crossing for an informed activist's view of the text as it has developed. But my greatest debt is to a policy practitioner, Peta Colebatch, who has for many years shared with me her enormous experience and understanding of the policy process, and who has now read the entire draft of three editions closely and critically, and made many constructive suggestions. To her, and to all those who have supported me in this intellectual journey, I offer my warmest thanks.

Why Worry About It?

Marrickville Council has approved a brothel on Marrickville Road despite concerns from some councillors [that] the brothel is located 40m from St Clement's Anglican Church. ...

Several councillors claimed it was council's policy to consider a brothel's proximity to a church when deciding an application. ...

At the meeting, Mayor Barry Cotter said the council had no policy to stop the brothel operating ...

He said if council refused the application it would be throwing away $15,000 of ratepayers' money in a court case doomed to fail.

(*The Glebe* [Sydney], 26 February 1997)

'Policy' is an idea that we use in both the analysis and the practice of the way we are governed. It gives both observers and participants a handle on the process, a way of making sense of the complex processes of governing. For people engaged in the practice of governing (as in the example quoted above), policy can be critically important. Here, the Mayor was warning his fellow councillors that if the case went to appeal, and they had refused approval on the basis of a clear policy (by which he meant, a formal statement of the rules and principles that the council follows), then the court would probably support the council's decision, but if there were no policy, the council's decision would probably be reversed.

So, while it is a concept in the social sciences, it is not 'owned' by social scientists. A wide range of participants in public life – public officials, elected representatives, community activists, scientific experts, journalists and others – use the term in their attempts to shape the way public life is organized. A student buys a motor scooter and finds that the policy of the highways department requires that she attend a training course before she can get a licence to drive it; the university's parking policy allows her to park it in only a few designated (and probably inconvenient) places on the campus; and when she shops around for insurance, many of the companies she contacts say, 'Sorry, we don't insure motor cycles or scooters; company policy.' All of these people are using 'policy' to shape the way they and other people behave.

For this student, policy seems to be about other people making life difficult for her. The other people would probably see it as about making life orderly and producing good outcomes: fewer scooter accidents, a neater-looking campus, less risk for the insurance company. For some public figures, policy is a lever against the inertia of the processes of government. The British cabinet minister Richard Crossman said that elected leaders need to have their ideas about what they are going to do enshrined in an election policy manifesto in order to strengthen their hand in their dealings with the bureaucracy after they have won the election. So policy can act as a vehicle for control: elected leaders over bureaucrats, central bureaucrats over field staff, company headquarters over operating managers, counter staff over customers. Counter staff in field offices may prefer there to be a central policy so that they are protected from having to exercise their own judgement: 'I'm not saying that you're not a good driver; it's company policy that I can't sell you the insurance you need.'

For other participants, policy may be a vehicle for contesting the existing order and asserting a right to participate. The existence of environment policy is not a result of some disembodied being called 'the government' identifying a problem and deciding how to deal with it; rather, it is the result of activity by concerned people – some inside the machinery of government, but most outside it – to draw attention to a range of things that were happening – air pollution, soil erosion, rivers silting up – and to have them recognized as part of a problem called 'the environment', which demanded a new approach. Calling for a policy on the environment (or equal employment opportunity, or urban traffic, or the use of information technology) is a way of challenging the existing policy agenda and the people who maintain it, and demanding the admission of new topics and new participants. For organized interests, the possibility of policy in their area can be a vehicle for their participation in the discussion. For participants inside government, policy development may give them some leverage against other arms of government. Establishing a national competition policy in Australia was seen as giving the Federal Government some leverage against the state governments, and also as giving state premiers some leverage against their own agencies.

Calls for policy may also reflect concern to shift the focus from process to content: from customary routines to the effect that they have. Drafting a homework policy in a school may enable a range of people – classroom teachers, parents, principals, students – to talk about what they see as the place of homework in education; there will probably be discussion of alternatives, the views of 'the experts' may be brought in, and the statement of policy that comes out of the exercise is likely to say something about why we have homework as well as how many hours students are expected to do. The growing interest in policy reflected an increasingly 'problem-oriented' approach to public business, with the discussion being shaped not in terms of the routines of particular agencies but in terms of the broad problem: 'flood control', 'homeless children', 'road accidents'. Organizations and individuals from inside and outside of government will be interested in the issue, and there may be formal structures for involving them, and for mobilizing expertise. So while 'policy' might be seen to close off debate and participation, making policy (and changing it) can be a vehicle for a wider range of players to enter the game.

But while 'policy' offers a useful handle on the process of governing, both for the observer and for the participant, it is not the only handle available to them. 'Management' is another way of explaining the steering of organizations, and for a time it seemed almost to eclipse 'policy' completely, as the language of business administration was applied to government, with calls to 'let the managers manage', and contentious areas of governing, such as the use of rivers, being addressed with 'management plans'. More recently, the favoured term has been 'governance', which recognizes that there is likely to be a wide range of participants involved in the response to public problems. The significance of these different terms will be discussed in more detail in Chapter 6; here, it is sufficient to note that 'policy' is not a distinct and unambiguous thing, but a way of labelling the action which makes sense to the participants, and that there are other ways of labelling that are also in use.

The discussion of policy has tended to centre on government, and it might be asked if 'policy' is something that happens only in government. Certainly, it is a term which we associate with government more than with business firms or non-governmental organizations. But, as we have seen, 'policy' is used by both firms and non-governmental organizations, particularly in mediating their relationships with the world 'outside'. Business firms find it important to have policies about the environmental impact of their activities. Universities need to have policies about the handling of student grievances. Church-run schools find themselves having to devise policy about whether teachers have to be members of the church. So we need to keep an open mind on how important policy is in any particular setting.

We have been speaking of 'policy' as such, but the discussion of policy tends to be more specific. It is more common to find references to 'public policy', usually meaning 'the activity of governments'. Then there is the full range of what we could call 'adjectival policy': health policy, transport policy, regional policy, environmental policy, etc. Here the focus is on the subject matter and how the structures of public authority deal with it. More will be said about this use of policy in later chapters, but the approach of this book is to locate 'policy' in a 'generic' perspective: it is concerned not with any particular policy field but with the idea of policy itself and the way it is used to shape, to explain and to validate the process of governing. In this way, it seeks to illuminate the ways in which attention is focused and the forms of public authority that are brought to bear, both in particular fields and more generally.

It is important to note that we say 'ways', not 'way': policy means different things to different people. Not only will participants and observers have different perspectives, but participants from different positions in the action are likely to see the same scene in different ways. Imagine a taskforce charged with developing policy on school dropouts and comprising representatives of the principals' association, the curriculum development unit of the education department, the parents' federation, an industry-backed vocational training body, and a coalition of youth activists. It is not that they would have different ways to answer the question; rather, they would have different questions. So the policy process involves not simply the pursuit of shared goals but also the more difficult task of constructing a basis for collective action among participants with quite diverse views on the nature of the task.

The approach we are taking is sometimes called the social construction perspective on policy: it sees policy as something that has to be constructed and sustained by the participants in circumstances where they are likely to have some degree of choice about how much to cooperate with others, which interpretive map to use and which cues to follow. It draws on work in a range of the social sciences, such as sociology, social psychology, organizational analysis, all of which ask 'what makes for collective action?', because this is the question to be answered. What this approach has to offer will become clearer as the book progresses; it is at variance with (though not necessarily opposed to) the two mainstream approaches in the writing about policy:

- The 'policy cycle' approach, which sees policy as a logical succession of stages, for example, definition of problem, identification of alternative responses, evaluation of options, decision, implementation (Parsons 1995: 77; see also Bridgman and Davis 2000: 27).
- 'Policy analysis' in the American style, which is concerned with the development of a methodology for determining the outcome of a specific course of action and for making comparisons between alternative courses of action in terms of their likely outcomes (see Jenkins-Smith 1990).

These perspectives are important in the construction of policy, and we will be paying attention to the way that they are mobilized by the participants, but we will not use them as the basis for our own exploration.

This book is addressed to a range of readers, including both practitioners and observers. There are those who are interested in a particular field (such as the environment) and want to know what it means to have 'environmental policy', and how that policy is produced. There are students of the political process, who want to know how 'policy' (or 'public policy') relates to well-established analytical terms such as 'politics', 'rule-making' or 'decision'. And then there are those who are interested in the broader issue of the way in which we are governed, which seems to mean more than just 'what the government decides to do', and to be concerned with the way that diverse activities by different bodies are drawn together into stable and predictable patterns of action which (as often as not) come to be labelled 'policy'.

So the book is a 'generic' guide to policy as such, rather than an introduction to any specific sort of policy. Policy is encountered in a wide range of contexts – different fields of action, different political systems and cultures, different times and circumstances – and it would be impossible to cover them all. The examples I have given are usually fictitious ones, constructed to make sense to readers from as wide a range of backgrounds and experiences as possible, but these have been supplemented with examples from practice, and with a chapter discussing how particular policy issues have been dealt with in one country. The book is structured around a series of straightforward questions which aim to clarify how the concept of policy gives us a fix on the action. Inevitably, in a book of this size, not much can be said about any particular aspect of the complex world of policy, but this is a set of questions about policy rather than a set of answers.

Further reading

There is an enormous amount of writing about policy, though in much of it, what the term means is assumed rather than explored. A comprehensive guide to the literature is Wayne Parsons's systematic and encyclopaedic *Public Policy: An Introduction to the Theory and Practice of Policy Analysis* (1995). This can be supplemented by three recent collections, all incorporating a range of approaches to policy: Peters and Pierre (2006), Goodin *et al.* (2006) and Fischer *et al.* (2007). This academic reading should be supplemented by paying close attention to the 'ordinary' use of the word, when references are made to 'policy' in company documents, public statements, judicial decisions, club newsletters, press releases, or whenever the term is used. In all of these cases, we can ask: What is meant by 'policy' here? Where does it come from? What do people do because of 'policy'? And why? These are the questions that will be explored in the course of this book.

2

What's the Idea?

The term 'policy' keeps appearing in our talk about the way we are governed. A scandal about the abuse of children by their carers leads to questions about the government's child protection policy. Experts in climate or land use or air quality organize their knowledge as an agenda of concern for government: a contribution to the making of 'environmental policy'. Uncertainty and discontent among teachers, students and parents over how much work students should do outside the classroom spur a high school to frame a 'homework policy'. The term seems to mean something broader than simply 'what the government wants to do'. It becomes part of everyday practice, as, for example, when a university secretary says, 'No, you can't email your essay, it has to be submitted in hard copy: departmental policy.' Here, using the term 'policy' justifies the action being taken: I am not interested in the case that you can make, and in fact I'm not really making a choice: I'm simply following policy.

Although (or perhaps because) the term has such a broad appeal, it does not have a clear and unambiguous definition. 'Policy' may be used to mean a broad orientation ('we have a policy of openness in government'), an indication of normal practice ('company policy is to buy from local suppliers where possible'), a specific commitment ('there has been a policy decision that analogue transmission will be phased out in favour of digital at the end of 2010'), or a statement of values ('honesty is the best policy'). The fact that 'policy' is used in so many ways is not necessarily a problem. In this book, we will not assume that 'policy' has a single meaning, but will try to clarify the way in which the term is used, and to illuminate the nature of different usages. For instance, do practitioners (who see much of their work as relating to policy – framing policy, advising on policy, negotiating changes to policy) – use the term in the same way as academic observers? We will be asking what 'policy' means without assuming that it always has the same meaning in all contexts.

That the term is so widely used suggests that the idea of 'policy' has a wide appeal, which leads to its being mobilized in a range of situations. It is part of the framework of ideas through which we make sense of the way in which, in different dimensions of our lives, we are governed. Governing does not just happen: it is constructed out of an array of shared ideas, categories, practices and organizational forms. 'Policy' is a way of labelling thoughts about the way the world is and the way it might be, and of justifying practices and organizational arrangements, and the participants in the governmental process seek to have their concerns and activities expressed as 'policy'. Feminists call for 'equal employment policies'; free-market advocates call for a national competition policy. The term carries a lot of symbolic power: for the participants, being able to mobilize the concept 'policy' matters, and we have to ask why this is so.

What is implied by 'policy'?

We should ask, first, what it is about 'policy' that gives it force? What are people using it to mean? We can identify (at least in contemporary western discourse about policy) three underlying themes: order, authority and expertise. These themes may be drawn on in varying degrees in different contexts, but they are part of a base of shared understandings on which talk about 'policy' rests.

First of all, 'policy' suggests order. Policy implies system and consistency. The action is not arbitrary or capricious: it is governed by a known formula of universal application. In this way, policy is seen to set limits on the behaviour of officials; at the same time, it frees them from the need to make choices. Moreover, it draws a range of activities into a common framework: we don't just impose punishments on unruly students, we apply a discipline policy.

In this context, a major source of difficulty is the problem of consistency between different policy fields. The policy of the highways agency on building urban freeways may clash with the policy of the wildlife agency on protecting the habitat of the native fauna. The policy of the water authority to extend its supply network may be at variance with the policy of the planning authority to contain the geographical spread of the city. Such inconsistencies are seen as a major policy problem, and much policy work is concerned with the way different agencies handle the same policy issues.

Secondly, policy implies authority. To speak of something as policy implies that it has the endorsement of some authorized decision-maker. It is the authority which legitimates the policy, and policy questions flow to and from authority figures: the minister, the director-general, the general manager, the executive committee. These figures may have little to do with the framing of policy, but policy draws on their authority, cascading down through the organization via the principle of hierarchy.

Thirdly, policy suggests expertise. Policy is seen as a process of governing some particular problem area, and this implies knowledge, both of the problem area and of the things that might be done about it. Policy knowledge is subdivided into functional areas: education policy, transport policy, etc. – the stress being on education or transport rather than on policy. When new policy concerns appear, such as the environment or equality of opportunity in employment, they are driven initially by widely shared principles, but over time, a body of specialized policy expertise is developed. And since this perspective sees policy as an exercise in skilled problem-solving, it invites the question 'does the policy work?', which generates a further specialized field of policy evaluation.

To say that order, authority and expertise are themes underlying the way policy is used is not to imply that they are all equally present at all points in the process. In fact, they may operate against one another; for instance:

- The desire of the minister for education to exercise her right to make a decision about the school-leaving examination (authority) may jeopardize the shared understandings so laboriously built up among schools, teachers, parents, universities, etc. (order).
- The criminologists know from careful research that taking a tough line on crime is not very effective (expertise), but find that the politicians think that the electorate favours this, and are more interested in the votes than the evidence (authority).
- Officials have negotiated a policy development which would be supported by all the relevant players (order), but the experts are

insisting on a controlled trial before they give it their support (expertise).

So policy outcomes are likely to embody a continuing tension between these attributes. And the underlying implications of 'policy' in cultural and political contexts outside the western liberal democratic origins of the term are a question which needs to be addressed, but this cannot be done in this short book.

Policy, governing and government

Policy has to do with governing, and it would be easy to assume that it is essentially about government. When problems arise, people often look to government to solve them, and 'policy' and 'public policy' become almost indistinguishable. It is assumed that governments choose policy objectives, policy is what governments decide to do, and policy must therefore be public. But here again, we can see that this way of thinking rests on some shared assumptions, not necessarily explicit. Perhaps the most fundamental one is instrumentality: that government is there to accomplish known objectives, particularly the solution of social problems. Politicians identify problems and what should be done about them, and claim credit (or evade blame) for the outcomes. So the work of government is seen as identifying and solving (or at least managing) problems by means of explicit courses of action – its policies. The problems may be fairly broadly stated ('youth unemployment') or be more specific ('the work relevance of the senior secondary curriculum'), they may change over time and place, and the goals may be more or less clearly stated, but policy is to be understood in terms of problems and solutions. Of course, in situations which are not seen as the government's concern (e.g. relationships within the family) or where government is seen as inept or corrupt, people may not link 'problem' to 'government'.

Other assumptions follow from this. One we could call coherence: all the bits of the action should fit together and form part of an organized whole, a single system; things should form part of a 'big picture'. The actions of teachers, welfare agencies, medical staff and police should all form part of a concerted effort to protect children at risk of abuse: the 'child protection policy'. Policy, in this context, has to do with how this system is (or should be) steered. This is an assumption which rests on its inherent value more than on the experience of the participants, for whom coherence is not so much one of the attributes of policy as one of the central problems: how to get all the different elements to focus on the same question in the same way. On the ground, governing looks less like a single-minded exercise of choice, and more like a pattern of interaction between different participants, a process of 'pulling and hauling', in which the different players try to shape activity in ways which reflect their particular perspectives. But coherence maintains its normative power: it should not be that the ministry of agriculture is helping farmers to grow tobacco while the ministry of health is trying to get people to stop smoking. So a lot of policy activity is concerned with 'coordination', i.e. mobilizing the value of coherence in an attempt to change what other participants do.

Another assumption is hierarchy: that governing is accomplished by the application of authority, with people at the top making decisions, giving instructions, and taking responsibility for them being carried out. This is an important part of the validation of action: that it is seen as flowing from the decisions of leaders with authority, and so acts of governing are explained by reference back to visible choices of these leaders ('decisions'). If other people (such as bureaucrats, organized interest or technical experts) are involved, they are said to be 'advising' the authority figure, or 'lobbying'. There is a sense of a central nervous system of public authority, which decides on a course of action and communicates it down the line. Authority flows downwards, and action must be seen to flow the same way.

There is also a shared assumption about the power of expertise: the work of governing is about managing problematic areas of social practice, and this requires drawing on specialist knowledge about these areas and their problems, and possible responses to these problems. This underlay the upsurge in policy studies in the second half of the twentieth century, from Lasswell's (1951) call for a 'policy science' and Wildavsky's (1979) confident assertion that the function of policy analysis is 'speaking truth to power'. At a more specific level, this has given rise to what we have called 'adjectival policy': the development of expertise focused on the areas of practice to be governed, such as health policy, transport policy, immigration policy.

Because 'policy' tends to be used to refer to what happens in government, its application outside government is less apparent. But the departmental policy on late essays, the church's policy on

foreign investments, or the mining company's policy on environmental protection are all uses of the term by non-governmental
bodies. Certainly, the term 'policy' is less common in business settings than in government. Although the term is sometimes
encountered, there is not a great field of 'business policy' to set
against 'public policy'. The direction of business firms is more likely
to be described by terms such as 'strategy' and 'corporate plans'. To
some extent, steering business firms is seen as less problematic than
steering government, perhaps reflecting the assumption that these
firms have the clear purpose of making a profit, the only question
being the way they might choose to do this, which makes statements
of policy unnecessary.

Where the term 'policy' does seem to be more commonly
employed in business is in stating practice to audiences outside the
firm, as in 'the policy of this firm is to recruit from the local community wherever possible'. Here, the statement is, in a sense, not
only a description of practice but also a justification of it. This
would suggest that we are more likely to find business firms making
statements about their policies in areas where outsiders have an
interest: for instance, firms might state their environmental protection policy, or their policy on equal employment opportunity.
They are less likely to describe the decision to seek an export market
for a product as a policy.

In the same way, the term 'policy' is less widely used in non-
commercial non-governmental organizations. In a voluntary association – e.g. a community child care centre, a church or a soccer
club – participants are unlikely to see themselves as being there to
accomplish policy objectives. But the use of 'policy' becomes more
common as the organization becomes more established, for reasons
which are worth noting. The child care centre, for instance, might
have started without many statements about what its objectives
were, other than 'to care for children'. But the centre might have
found it necessary to decide what to do about children who were
sick: the staff might have found that sick children could not participate in the normal activities and that it was difficult to care for
them without neglecting the other children. The parents of the other
children might have complained that their children were getting sick
as a consequence of sick children being allowed to continue
attending the centre. There might have been concerns from the
public health authorities, and the centre staff might have found out
that schools had a standard response to illness, excluding children

with specified ailments for prescribed periods of time. The centre might then have defined its own sickness policy so that the staff and parents did not have to decide and negotiate each case as it came up.

We can see here that 'policy' can mean not a set of objectives for the activity, or even the guiding principles, but simply the standardization and articulation of practice: 'this is the way we do it here'. The adoption of such policies by the centre is likely to reflect a number of processes: the centre is growing and the director wants to be sure all the staff do the same thing; increasingly, the staff have had training and want to supervise activities, not care for sick children; staff will become aware of practice in other centres, perhaps through an association of child care centres; and regulatory officials may be asking increasingly specific questions about practice. In other words, articulating policy in organizations has to do with looking sideways ('who are the relevant others, and what are they doing?') as well as with looking forward ('where do we want to go?').

In this example, we can see the emergence of policy within organizations seen as 'non-governmental'; we can also find non-governmental organizations being drawn into governmental policy activity. For example, the child care centre's policy on children's illnesses and attendance would not have been developed solely within the centre. The construction of policy involves more than just government: other participants have a significant role to play, particularly in the impact they have on which things are seen as problems and worthy of policy attention. Even if we stick to the perception that it is governments that 'make policy', it is clear that they do not make it in times and circumstances of their own choosing, and non-government is also an important part of the policy process. A range of people and organizations that are concerned about the governing of particular areas of practice engage in a continuing struggle to mobilize the concept of 'policy' as part of their activities: proclaiming it, contesting it, transforming it, or simply assuming it.

Choice and structure

Discussion of policy often refers to 'policy-makers', implying that policy is the creation of authorized leaders, the product of the choices that these leaders have made. This is the way in which these

leaders would describe policy: it is their job to make policy decisions, and there are also jobs for others, advising them about the
decisions they ought to make, and carrying out the policies once
the decision has been made. But this does not give us an adequate
analysis of the policy process.

One reason is that it sometimes seems difficult to divide the
action into clear policy decisions, on the one hand, and action taken
to carry them out, on the other. As Schaffer and Corbett (1965: xiii)
put it, we do not find 'policy' as a thing apart, 'existing on a
somewhat airless plateau', and quite distinct from 'a jumble of
activities among the lower foothills'. Rather, it is a point of relative
firmness built into a continuing flow: 'an obligation for some, a
structural factor for other participants'.

The 'choice' assumption is that this 'point of relative firmness' is
created when a leader (or group of leaders) who is authorized to do
so, chooses to do something. Often, people can indicate a point in
time at which a person or collective body approved a document
setting out a course of action, and see this as the choice that made
the policy. But this decision is likely to have had its origin in
practice – what can be done conveniently and systematically?, what
worked last time?, what is consistent with the expectations that
others have of us? – which shaped what has been sent up the line for
endorsement. In other words, the proposal reflects the concerns and
practices of the structure that generated it. The endorsement may
have been given by those in authority, but they may have had little
interest in it, or even have been against it, but not to the point of
open opposition. Therefore, while it may be legally correct to
describe this endorsement as their 'decision', this may not tell us
much about how this outcome was reached.

In any case, many would argue that having a formal policy
decision is only the beginning of the policy process, and the critical
thing is what happens as a consequence. It is easy to say 'It is
company policy to care for the environment', but does anything
change as a result? What resources are allocated to environmental
care? Are any staff allocated to the task? What happens when there
is a clash between maintaining production and caring for the
environment? For this reason some would argue that policy has to
be understood in terms not of intent but of commitments.

> I shall use the term 'public policy' to refer to the substance of what
> government does; to the pattern of resources which they actually

commit as a response to what they see as public problems or challenges warranting public action for their solution or attainment. ... I
do not pretend that all students of public policy would agree with the
meaning which I attach to this term, but then I do not consider that
goals, intentions, principles, decisions, wishes, objectives or anything
else that has been seen as constituting a public policy represents an
appropriate usage of the term.

(Dearlove 1973: 2)

In this perspective, policy must be understood not simply in terms
of officially proclaimed goals, but in terms of the way that activity
among a wide range of participants is patterned, so that people
know what is going to happen. Goal statements may be significant,
but they are unlikely to tell the whole story, and their absence does
not mean that there is no policy. The players in the game learn how
things are done, they learn how the world is viewed, what is
regarded as the problem, and what can be done about it.

This points to the importance of the 'knowledge base' in which
the participants are operating. What matters are appropriate subjects for collective action? And what bodies of knowledge are seen
as appropriate for discussing them? Should governments be concerned about child-rearing practices? Should companies be
concerned about their impact on the local economy? Should a
church-run welfare agency be concerned about the career progression of its paid staff? Here, occupations are an important source of
pattern. If the welfare agency has a director of employee relations
with training and experience in human resource management, it is
more likely that the agency will have policy on career development
than if it is run by people with a strong religious background but
little experience in personnel management. Different occupations
make sense of the action in different ways: a production engineer
and a wildlife biologist will know quite different things about a
proposal to extend a factory into adjoining woodland, and are
likely to reach quite different conclusions about whether it is consistent with the statement 'It is company policy to care for the
environment'. In this perspective, the essential thing about policy is
not the aspirations but the effect they have on the action: policy is,
in Schaffer's words, 'a structured commitment of important
resources' (1977: 11).

So we are seeing structure – how we are organized, how we think
and talk about the task, what we are trained and skilled at doing –
as much as choice, particularly if this is taken to mean 'selecting

from among alternative courses of action'. So we want to know what shapes this commitment of important resources, and where (and when) do the preferences of the 'policy-makers' come into the picture. Of course, making statements about policy goals is one of the important ways of committing resources, but it may not be sufficient, and it is certainly not the only way. The most important form of commitment is inertia: what we did last year is the best guide to what we will do this year. The budget tends to express this commitment, and carry it forward from year to year. The organization chart represents a particular commitment of resources: having a department of agriculture or a consumer affairs bureau or an office of small business reflects recognition of these interests, and offers a base for further claims. All of these would have to be counted as part of the structured commitment of important resources.

What we can see here is an ambiguity in the concept of policy: a tension between choice and structure. To describe policy as the choices of authorized decision-makers implies that the action follows from the decision: they could have chosen something else, and different action would have followed. But the experience of the policy process is often that it is the flow of action which throws up the opportunities for choice, and that the scope for choice is limited by the action already in place and the commitments which it embodies. For example, if there is an established system of technical schools, there will be decisions to be made about budgets and staff levels and new facilities, but it would be difficult to decide that vocational education should be conducted in the workplace rather than in schools. So much has already been committed to the system of technical schools – there are buildings and specialized staff and graduates who do not want the worth of their qualifications to be questioned – that it would be very difficult to close the schools down completely. It would not be impossible, but it would require enormous effort. Over time, policy innovations become institutionalized – in the form of bricks and mortar, the names of organizations and in job titles – and the commitment to maintaining them becomes very strong,

So the demands for decision-making emerge from the existing system, and the scope for choice is limited by the commitments that have been built upon previous choices. And in this case, the initial choice might have been an agreement a century ago to pay a small stipend to a couple of part-time instructors at one school. And that decision may well have been generated by the flow of action: for instance, the employers might have been doing the training themselves but decided that they would like to pass this responsibility to some public authority, and the relevant decision-maker agreed to provide the relatively small sum involved, on the basis that this was consistent with other forms of public support for education. The large system of technical schools was built on this very small foundation. A choice was made then, but it was not a choice to have the outcome which we now see; this is an example of what is called 'path dependency'.

This is also an example of the inherent tension between agency and structure. People act (agency), but their actions are significant only in the context of a set of relationships (structure), and this limits the actions that they can meaningfully take. Giddens (1984) argued that we have to see agency and structure as mutually constituting one another. Structure indicates an appropriate way to act; when people act that way, their action reproduces the structure. For instance, because farmers have been politically valued, there may be an agency for farmers within government, and in the event of, say, a drought, this agency may press for special assistance for the farmers affected. If assistance is given (action), this act reinforces the strength of the farming interest within the political system (structure). On the other hand, if the aid is refused because rainfall fluctuations are seen as normal and part of the business environment of the farmer (action), this weakens the farmers' claim to special consideration (structure).

The point here is not that structure gets in the way of choice: the two dimensions of the policy process are inextricably linked to one another. Unless the policy decision could shape the action, there would be no point in making it. Unless the action could be linked to some policy statement, it would be difficult to secure support for it. But the two dimensions operate against one another: making choices challenges the existing structure, and having this structure limits the opportunity for choice. So there is a structural tension between the two in the policy process, and, as a consequence, a lot of ambiguity.

As this example suggests, one of the most important elements of structuring in policy is specialized forms of organization. When issues are recognized as matters of public concern, organizations tend to emerge within government to deal with them – e.g. the Department of Agriculture, the Environmental Protection Agency, the War Veterans Administration. These bodies develop specialist knowledge of that field of action and of the participants in it and their concerns, and they tend to become (and are expected to be) the voice of that interest within government. So policy action in relation to agriculture, for instance, will be shaped by the knowledge and orientation of the department, the understanding it has of other participants (such as farmers' organizations) and their preferences, and the department's need for their continuing cooperation – 'the shadow of the future', as it has been called.

But action within government often concerns more than one agency, and the different agencies are likely to see such action through their own perceptual lenses. Consider, for instance, the following example. The management of a suburban shopping mall were concerned about the large number of noisy, boisterous teenagers hanging around the mall and called the police to evict them. The arrival of the police inflamed the teenagers, punches were thrown, arrests were made, and the incident was given extensive coverage on the TV news that night, with opposition politicians demanding that the government define its policy on young people and shopping malls.

'The government' here has many heads. Some shopping malls are owned by the Public Service Superannuation Fund, which wants to keep the teenagers out because it fears they will discourage other shoppers from coming to the mall. The police recognize the tension in the air, and they think that if they wanted to, they could probably find some offence to charge these young people with, but do not really see this as a 'law and order' matter and would prefer that teenagers basically cooperate with police rather than oppose them. The education department (which was also drawn in) is primarily concerned with whether the young people involved should have been at school that day, and the local council's community development department sees this as evidence of a need for more recreation activities for young people and would like money to be allocated to create them. The Children's Commission (an agency recently established by government) is investigating this as a possible example of adult harassment of children and denial of their rights.

In this case, the nature of the policy response will depend on 'who gets the ball' – which agency is seen as being responsible, and how the story is told. Is this about policing? Social development? Urban design? The rights of stigmatized groups? And clearly, there is an interplay between how the problem is defined and who gets the job of dealing with it. The structure is not given in advance: it emerges from the interplay among the participants. Defining the problem as the shortage of recreation activities means that people look to the community development department for an answer, and it can then make claims on resources to create these activities. The choices that are available have been structured by the way the problem is viewed and by whose job it is to do something about it.

Policy and labelling

What we are seeing here is that 'policy' is a construct in practice, a term used by practitioners in shaping the action as well as by academic observers trying to make sense of it. This makes it difficult to start with a clear definition of what the term means; we have to ask what it is used to mean (and, in turn, to be clear about what we ourselves mean by it). 'Policy' is a word which frames the action rather than simply describes it: it labels what we see so that we can make sense of it in a particular way. For a start, it describes the process of governing in a particular way, stressing order, intention and outcome, and this makes the practice valid. As the Mayor told the councillors in our opening example (p. 1), making a choice that is not consistent with policy may result in the decision being overruled.

Furthermore, the labelling directs our attention in particular ways. To say 'our policy on the young unemployed is in total disarray' is to highlight some things rather than others – e.g. young unemployed people as such, rather than on the supply of jobs or the state of the economy – and to assume that the activities of different agencies (e.g. those responsible for education, social security, employment, policing, human rights) should be consistent with one another, and directed towards the solution of the identified problem (in this case, the position of young unemployed people).

At the same time, the labelling directs attention away from other dimensions of the action. It directs attention to young unemployed rather than older unemployed, or young apprentices. It focuses attention on the implications for the young unemployed of the activities of schools or the police. But these agencies might see their primary task as being to run a system of universal education, or to keep the peace and apprehend lawbreakers, and look upon the situation of the young unemployed as a side issue. To talk about 'policy on the young unemployed' is to frame the action in such a way as to make it a central issue rather than a side issue.

To state that 'policy' is a particular way of framing the action implies that there are alternatives – and there certainly are. Perhaps the most obvious is 'politics'; 'administration' or 'management' or 'strategy' would be others. The distinction between these terms will be discussed in more detail in Chapter 5, but we can note here that in ordinary usage, 'politics' seems to denote a continuing struggle for partisan advantage, whereas 'policy' implies a settled, considered choice, and 'administration' the execution of these choices. 'Management' (like 'strategy', 'corporate planning' and 'vision') is a term which originally was mostly used in business, but in recent years has become widely used in government and non-profit organizations. Many would claim that it is not really an alternative to policy but is simply concerned with the ways in which policy objectives can be efficiently and effectively pursued. Others would argue that, in practice, the stress on 'letting the managers manage' means an increase in the autonomy of managers and a reduction in the scope of authority figures to determine policy.

Perhaps the main alternative to policy as a way of framing the world might not even be recognized as a label: we could call it 'practice'. People do things in ways that make sense to them, and there is no formal prescription about how they should act: they have operational autonomy. The existence of this sort of autonomy is sometimes overlaid and reinforced by claims about professional expertise: that it is inappropriate to have policies which override professional judgement. For instance, if a student threatens a teacher with a knife, should this student automatically be suspended, or should the decision be left to the professional judgement of the school staff? Teachers may prefer to be able to use their own judgement, but officials of the education department would feel more secure if there was a standard practice which all teachers followed: a policy.

In all of this, we are seeing the way in which policy expresses relationships of power. The formal 'decision-making' in which leaders enunciate and validate courses of action is an expression of their power. The interplay among participants to define the issue operates to recognize the legitimate participants and their right to influence the allocation of resources. And power is also expressed in the shared understandings and values which underlie the exercise of public authority (e.g. whether personal practices in relation to smoking and diet are matters of public concern). This will be discussed further in the next chapter, but we need to note here that in talking about policy, we are talking about power.

Policy as a concept in use

This discussion has gone some way beyond the common-sense understanding of policy as a thing: a clearly stated (or at least generally understood) statement of intent on behalf of the organization: e.g. 'our policy on the level of immigration'.

Certainly, policy in this sense is (or can be) important, but we need to go beyond this. If statements like this are significant, it is because of the extent to which they shape practice. We need to ask what shapes practice, and how does the idea of policy play a part in this? This directs our attention to who the participants are, the locations in which they interact with one another, and the discourses that are used in giving pattern and stability to the action.

We have seen in this chapter that the concept of policy mobilizes particular values. It expresses values of instrumental rationality and of legitimate authority. It presents action in terms of the collective pursuit of known goals, so that it becomes stable and predictable. And it sees these goals as being determined by some legitimate authority.

In doing this, the concept of policy both explains and validates the action: it explains what people are doing, and it makes it appropriate for them to do it. So it is not simply a descriptive term: it is a concept in use, and understanding 'policy' means understanding the way in which practitioners use it to shape the action.

But it is also a concept in use for observers: we use it as a way of interrogating organized activity – particularly, but not exclusively, in relation to public authority. It leads us to ask who is involved, in what settings, how action is framed, and what is the significance in this process of the idea of authorized purpose: that is, to ask questions about policy as a process, and not simply an outcome.

Further reading

Most of the writing about policy does not give a great deal of attention to the conceptual questions underlying the term. It is clear that ideas about organization are important in perceptions of policy, and Gareth Morgan's *Images of Organization* (1986) is helpful in clarifying these. Kaufman's *Are Government Organizations Immortal?* (1976) illustrates the tension between choice and structure, and March and Olsen's (1983) analysis of this point is very helpful. Schön and Rein (1994) draw attention to the way in which issues are 'framed'. Schmidt (1993) is a nice illustration of how different participants in the same process can know different things. It is also helpful to read some of the fine case studies of national differences in policy style, such as Dobbin (1994), Hendriks (1999), Héritier (1999) and the collections edited by Richardson (1982) and Fischer *et al.* (2007).

3
What's Going On?

In political thought and analysis, we have still not cut off the head of the king.

(Foucault 1986: 88–9)

It is as though there were a political gateway through which all issues pass. Disputed from the moment they are in sight of it – and more hotly as they approach – they pass (if they pass) through, and drop out of controversy for a time. Managing the procession are certain 'gatekeepers' – not just the Cabinet of the day, but bureaucrats, journalists, association heads and independent specialists camped permanently around each source of problems.

(Davies 1964: 3)

One of the most seductive terms in the study of policy is 'the policy-makers'. It has a clear ring to it and conveys an impression of a known group of evident and purposeful decision-makers deter-mining the course of action. But this is not necessarily the way that the people who are identified as policy-makers see it. They often report that they do not seem to be out on their own, making something; rather, they find themselves presiding over an extended array of people with varying levels of interest in the question and quite distinct perspectives on it. They may find that their own ability to determine the outcome is quite limited, and they might wonder if 'policy-making' is going on somewhere else. So their account of the policy process might be quite different from the vision of orderly problem-solving implied in references to 'policy-makers'.

If we dig deeper, we find that the visible bits of governing that we recognize as 'policy' often rest on foundations of understandings and practices that tend to be taken for granted. For instance, a policy that all school students should learn a certain amount of information technology (IT) rests on understandings, rules and expectations about school attendance, curriculum design, the way society is changing and the future needs for workplace skills. These foundations make the IT education policy possible, but they are not constructed for that reason. So if we want to understand policy in this area, we are driven to look at the way in which this foundation is shaped – for instance, the way that people come to recognize 'IT skills' as a matter of concern, and make demands about its place in the school curriculum (as compared, for instance, with skills in managing alcohol consumption, which may be equally important for the students but seen as having less of a claim on classroom time). Digging deeper still, we find the ways in which people construct rationales of action which make attendance at school, and receiving instruction there on IT, a sensible and acceptable way of meeting the need, and in this way make the IT policy possible. In this perspective, 'policy-making' about students and IT skills has to be traced back to the understandings and values of a wide range of significant people.

So there are several ways of giving an account of policy, which stress different aspects of the processes at work. Some accounts frame it in terms of choice by governments; others focus on the way that it emerges from the interplay of a range of stakeholders; other accounts draw attention to the way in which these activities are grounded in a bed of shared understandings, values and practices. Moreover, more than one account may be drawn upon in explaining and justifying what is happening. It is useful to identify each of these accounts in turn, and then to think about the ways in which they are used in analysis and in practice.

Authoritative choice: policy-making as deciding

Authoritative choice is the dominant, 'common-sense' account of policy: it is a process of choice by authorized decision-makers – 'the government' – who select courses of action which will maximize the values they hold, and transmit these to subordinate officials to implement. (It may be that the subordinate officials propose the courses of action, but the decision-makers still have to give their approval.) It is an account which stresses instrumental action, rational choice and the force of legitimate authority. It directs attention to the ability or capacity of subordinate officials to give effect to these decisions (the 'implementation problem') and to ways of structuring the process of government so as to achieve this compliance.

In this account, policy is described as the work of 'the authorities'. This may mean a single individual: 'the minister has decided ...' or 'the secretary-general had determined ...'; but often, it is a collective body which is seen as having authority: the cabinet, the board of directors, or the national council. Sometimes, it may be the members of the legislature which are seen as having the authority to make policy. Some writers, particularly in the United States, are inclined to see a policy as being expressed in a piece of legislation; it follows that the legislators who voted for this legislation are 'the policy-makers'. In Westminster systems (such as Australia, Canada or the UK), where the executive can usually count on party discipline to keep the legislators in line, this use of the term is less common (but see Jackson (1995) on the decline of executive control of parliaments). But there is still widespread concern that the courts may make decisions on policy matters which should be for the legislature to determine. It is the legislature which has the authority to decide. The courts (it is argued) should not pre-empt the authority of the legislature.

But, as we shall see, authority in government is not neatly concentrated at one point, but is diffused through the system. Even within a single government, work is divided among a range of specialist agencies. For instance, there will be agencies to build roads or run national parks or monitor greenhouse gas levels, and they may each have different views about a proposal to run a highway through a national park. There is usually some dispersal of authority to local and regional levels of government, though the extent of dispersal varies: in federal systems it is most pronounced and best protected, but even in unitary systems there is rarely a complete concentration of authority at the centre. And increasingly, policy activity is being carried out in international arenas, such as the European Union, or UN agencies such as the World Health Organization, and the World Trade Organization.

Although we may speak of the 'machinery of government', not all government organizations can be seen as simply the tools of the authorized leaders. The police, for instance, often have considerable autonomy and freedom from governmental direction. Other bodies need a degree of autonomy and freedom from central authority simply to operate. The courts, for instance, need to be independent of the government if they are to be seen as neutral arenas for dispute settlement. While universities may be publicly funded, they are loath to see themselves as the instruments of the governments which provide the funds. And though governments have often run trading enterprises such as railways or telecommunications services, these bodies are given considerable operational autonomy in order to insulate their commercial activity from political pressures.

But while there may be many organizations involved in exercising public authority, the authoritative choice account sees them all as being part of one system, exercising the will of 'the government'. This means that this account may not be an accurate description of what happens in 'policy-making', but, as we shall see, it may be 'a good account' for other reasons.

Structured interaction: policy-making as negotiating

We can see from the above discussion that making policy is likely to involve participants in different organizations, and these may be outwith the line of hierarchical authority. Policy participants recognize that much of their work takes place across organizational boundaries (or outside them) as well as within them, and their account of policy work is as much concerned with identifying other players and negotiating with them as it is concerned with selecting and pursuing goals. In this account, 'policy-making' is about relationships and linkage. In the example above of the highway through the national park, the question would be how the various participants were able to find ways to pursue their own agendas while recognizing the competing agendas of other players. The authoritative choice perspective would suggest that the officials concerned would go to the source of the authority – the cabinet – and secure endorsement for their activity, and this would then impose an authoritative outcome on all ministers and their officials. But research suggests that officials are relatively reluctant to go to cabinet to settle a dispute between departments until they have exhausted the possibility of negotiating their own agreement with other officials (Painter 1981), and that the cabinet would usually expect the officials concerned to work out a settlement and present it to cabinet for endorsement. So, officials will usually be trying to create order through negotiation with other participants, carrying the struggle into the cabinet room only over major issues.

This happens on the ground as well as at headquarters. For people lower down in the organization, the policy-making of the people at the top may not be sufficient to make their jobs stable and predictable, and they may have to construct some order themselves. 'Street-level bureaucrats' – i.e. those like magistrates in lower courts, schoolteachers and police, who are in direct contact with the clientele of the organization – will work out with the clientele and other relevant participants (e.g. lawyers) how the service will operate. So it can be argued that, at their own level, these people are also making policy (see Lipsky 1980). This is because policy is concerned with making organized activity stable and predictable. If, for instance, an education department has a policy that children are not allowed to start school until they are 5 years old, and if schools use this as the basis for enrolling new students, then the policy helps to avoid tension-filled encounters between school principals and anxious parents, and all the affected parties – children, parents, teachers, educational planners – know the situation. Creating this sort of order can be seen as a problem of organizational control: how to ensure that the policy which has been created at the top is carried out through the organization, and how to avoid, on the one hand, bureaucratic rigidity, and, on the other, excessive slack. But it is likely that there has been as much demand for the policy from below (e.g. school principals) as from above, as the principals try to manage the demands of their clientele.

This need to create order calls for interaction across a range of functionally defined organizations within government, e.g. those concerned with health, welfare, housing, transport. If a policy on aged care, for instance, is to generate predictability, it must involve these organizations. Constitutional divisions may create a need for interaction. The national government may take responsibility for transport, but leave health with regional governments subject to national guidelines; housing may be the responsibility of a public corporation not under direct governmental control; and welfare activity may be carried out by regional and local governments and by non-governmental bodies. In this context, the question is not simply 'who needs to be included?', but also 'who must not be left out?', i.e. whose exclusion would frustrate the policy or simply make it pointless?

But the interaction is not confined to government. The most important source of caring for the aged is the family, and a critical question is always, 'when an old person is in need of care, to what extent will that care be provided by members of the family?' But this depends on the family, which usually does not see itself as an organization: there is no National Association of Families to speak for the family in policy circles. This bring us to the social construction of the policy question: what are considered appropriate forms of conduct for family members (including the question of who are to be considered family members), and how are these articulated, communicated and enforced? This becomes particularly important when people from societies where social welfare is primarily a matter of family and obligation migrate to more secular, western societies with a tradition of state payments and entitlement.

In the above case, we can see that policy does not emerge from some detached being called 'the government' looking down and recognizing a problem; it emerges from the intersection of a number of players inside and outside government. For instance, a 75-year-old widow falls at home, breaks her hip and is taken to hospital, where she has a hip replacement. When the medical work is completed, the hospital wants to discharge her, but she is not yet able to look after herself at home. She could be transferred to an institution offering a lower level of care (whether governmental or nongovernmental) or looked after by family and friends. In the long run, she could perhaps look after herself at home if some changes were made to the house and she had some help for specific tasks, which might be given by family or neighbours, or by paid visiting helpers. What happens in this particular case will emerge from negotiations between the hospital, other institutions, local welfare authorities and the woman's family. In these negotiations, participants will look for rules and norms of practice, e.g. 'when medical treatment is completed, the patient becomes the responsibility of the welfare authorities', or 'the family is expected to care for its elderly members unless circumstances make this impossible', or 'old people who can afford to pay for their care are expected to do so'. Policy development is a process of creating order in problematic situations, and is likely to involve a number of hands, inside and outside government.

One consequence is that policy fields are likely to cut across organizational boundaries: indeed, they may have been created with this intention. In the aged policy case, there may be a commissioner for ageing, created by government specifically to have a concern for older people and to press other organizations to conduct themselves with the needs of older people in mind. As we saw in the discussion on expertise, the whole idea of environmental policy was a challenge to existing policy fields and the expertise on which they drew, and to compel the various players to think about their activities in terms of an overarching set of values. Heritage policy, equal employment opportunity policy or family policy would be other examples. They often originate outside the central policy framework – among community groups, professional associations, consultative bodies, etc. – and get support in part because they offer the prospect of a way of managing demands for an official response. If ministers find that they are always vulnerable to demands that they protect some historical building from development, they are likely to find considerable value in a heritage policy which to some extent defines and limits what can be expected of the government.

So new policy demands represent challenges to the existing order, and will probably be resisted at first: demands for the preservation of buildings because of their heritage value carry no weight in a policy order based on ownership rights and the principles of good planning. But if demonstrators take to the streets (perhaps sparked by the demolition of a familiar old building), consent authorities are swamped by objections, development projects are slowed down and company meetings are disrupted by protesters, then people in authority will seek to draw the dissidents into the policy order – setting up consultative machinery and amending the criteria for approval, and, in this way, restoring order by adding 'heritage' to the policy agenda.

A great deal of policy activity is concerned with creating and maintaining order among the diversity of participants in the policy process. It seems to be not so much about deciding, but more about negotiating. And the negotiations focus less on alternatives between which we must choose, and more on common ground on which we can converge. The process is likely to be fine-grained and long-running. The participants work out a resolution of one set of problems, but new problems replace them, and they mobilize their collective problem-solving skills to address the new problems.

Social construction: policy-making as collective puzzling

As we noted at the beginning of this chapter in the example of IT instruction in schools, making policy involves recognizing problems and appropriate answers to these problems. It is seen as appropriate that IT skills are taught in schools, but not necessarily skills in managing alcohol consumption. So as Heclo (1974) once put it, much of the policy process is concerned with 'collective puzzling', asking 'What is of collective concern? What is known about this? Who are the experts? What is normal and what is deviant? What is an appropriate response? What is the place of public authority in bringing this response to bear?'

This dimension of policy formation is perhaps hard to see because it is concerned with things that are often taken for granted. It seems 'common sense' that government is concerned with problems, and if government is dealing with something, it must be a problem. But we should be asking 'why is this a problem, but that not a problem?', or 'why is this a problem here but not there, or now but not before?', Policy formation rests on problematization: interpreting the world in a way that makes it appropriate to address particular situations in particular ways. How this is done may change. Today, governments in many industrial countries recognize 'homeless youth' as a policy problem, and policy attention is directed to creating appropriate forms of housing for these people. Fifty or more years ago, these people might have been called 'runaway children', and the policy response would be to apprehend them and return them to the parental home. So while we can see policy formation as 'problem-solving', it can also be seen as 'problem-finding': interpreting the world in a way that makes particular forms of organized response appropriate.

Viewing policy formation this way the question becomes 'how are problems and responses identified, and in what way is this challenged and changed?' What are the sorts of expertise which are drawn on? Expertise is not generic and free-floating, but has a specific focus: expertise about health, for instance, or welfare, or transport. This focus is sharpened by the nature of the institutional homes (as it were) for expertise: there is likely to be a government agency responsible for health, another for welfare, and another for transport. Responsibility for policy in any given area will be claimed by some functionally defined group of experts, and the experts in government will probably have good links with those outside. The institutional specialization we have noticed in government is matched in the universities (which locate their expertise in these fields in different departments, often in different faculties) and in professional organizations. Consequently, the health experts in government are likely to have established links with health experts in universities and professional organizations, and also with voluntary bodies, companies and international organizations. Moreover, their links with their fellow health experts are likely to be stronger than their links with, say, the transport experts in government.

Furthermore, the links run both ways. A company may respond to the emergence of environmental protection policy by establishing its own environmental protection branch, and would expect that its own experts would establish a good relationship with the environmental experts in government in order to get a better idea of the expectations of government and in the hope that the company's own concerns will be taken into account in the policy process. On the other side of the coin, the company's environmental experts could be expected to use their knowledge of the orientation of government to help them get attention within the company. When community groups demand a policy response on environmental problems, they look to the environmental experts in government for a sympathetic hearing, and one of the first demands of such groups is that there should be (if there is not one already) an environmental protection agency – an institutional location in government for their policy concern.

In this way, expertise becomes an important way of organizing policy activity. People who are concerned with a particular policy area develop a special knowledge about it, and come to know who shares that knowledge: who are the people that they can talk to about it. There may well be newspapers or journals which they all read, or associations to which they tend to belong. They may have different ideas about what to do about the problem, but they recognize that they are all addressing the same problem. So analysts of the policy process see them as a significant grouping in the policy process: an 'issue network' or 'policy community'.

But we cannot assume that for any and every policy question there is a single, obvious field of policy-relevant expertise. The care of frail old people, for instance, could involve a wide range of functional experts: in health, welfare, housing, transport – even taxation. Old people are more prone to illness, and often end up being kept in hospital because (as in the example just cited) they cannot cope by themselves at home. But with some help in the home, perhaps some renovations (e.g. replacing stairs with a ramp, installing handrails), they would be able to do so. But these diverse fields of expertise will focus what could be considered different aspects of the same question. For our 75-year-old lady with a broken hip, the concerns of the doctors are 'is there any treatment that we can provide?'; the hospital management will be asking 'is there a more appropriate (and cheaper) location for her?; the domiciliary care unit within the health service will be asking 'could we be given the responsibility (and the funding) to care for her in her own home?'; the community services section of the local council will be asking 'could we organize some combination of changes to the house and support services (paid or unpaid) which would enable her to continue living in her own home?'; and the family may be asking 'should we be taking responsibility for her?' The policy task may be how to mobilize the different sorts of expertise that are available. And some may argue that government involvement in the care opens up the possibility of an infinitely expanding demand for spending as the demographic pattern changes, and that the policy task is to resist these demands and to deflect the responsibility back to self-provision, family and community support.

This shows not only that there can be different expert answers to the same policy problem, but also that it cannot be assumed that it is the same problem. These different bodies of expertise are not so much generating responses to the problem as framing the problem in the first place. A body of expertise is a way of recognizing problems as well as a way of addressing them. And this is not a neutral process: it has implications for the allocation of resources. If the lady with the broken hip is seen as a medical problem, it is likely that funding will go to the hospital, or to another form of institutionalized care. If responsibility is transferred to the local welfare agency, the funding transferred (if any) is likely to be much less than the cost of hospital care – which may be a reason for financial managers in the ministry of health, or even the ministry of finance itself, to become interested in policy on the care of the frail aged.

Moreover, it may not simply be that the policy problem involves a number of the existing pools of expertise: there are times when we can see new expertise being developed to challenge the existing pattern of policy knowledge. Environmental policy offers a good example. Some people were concerned about the impact of social and economic change on what might be called the amenity of ordinary life, and this came to be referred to as 'the quality of the environment'. This was a new term for something which had previously been without a label, but it took root (not without resistance from the interests which were being challenged), and became part of 'ordinary knowledge'. There also emerged specialized knowledge: academic research and professional expertise about 'the environment'. This found an institutional home in the universities and in environmental protection agencies. As it became established, it was used to challenge both the expertise and the practices of the existing players. For instance, it became common to require an environmental impact statement for all new developments. This meant that engineers wanting to build a new road had to address themselves to a different question, and justify their plans in terms of a different body of expertise.

This brings us to ask which sorts of expertise can be mobilized in policy discussion. Many radical activists would argue that their policy ideas are not taken seriously and they are excluded from serious policy discussion. This has been taken further by researchers who have argued that by preventing issues being raised in this way, the powerful are able to maintain their dominance, through 'agenda control' and 'non-decisions'. At a deeper level, Lukes (1974) identifies a 'third dimension' of power, arguing that through the dominance of 'mainstream' ideas and symbols, the interests of the powerful are protected, and the powerless are marginalized, without any need for specific action.

For this reason, many analysts of the policy process have taken an 'interpretive' approach to policy, stressing that 'policy issues' are not naturally occurring, but are 'socially constructed' by the participants. These writers see policy as a discourse (Fischer and Forester 1993), and focus on how meaning is conveyed (Yanow 1996), and the ways that questions are 'framed' (Schön and Rein 1994) and argued (Majone 1989). They recognize that there is more than one framing (Roe 1994), that dominant framings can be contested, and that policy action often involves contest between frames (Throgmorton 1991). So, while the social construction perspective may take us into the depths of the taken-for-granted, it also points to the way in which contests over meaning are important in the framing of action. When Al Gore won the Nobel Peace Prize in 2007 for his policy advocacy on climate change, more than a few Democrats hoped that he might run for president again, but he would not be tempted, and one political commentator claimed that Gore had 'come to believe that even a US president is powerless to act on climate change unless public opinion has moved', and Gore had made a bigger policy impact as a teacher and advocate than George Bush had as president of the United States (Freedland 2007).

How the different accounts interact

We have identified three different accounts of policy: policy practitioners learn to recognize all of them, and to use the account that is most appropriate at the time. They know that the authoritative choice account is the 'sacred' account, and the right way to present the policy outcome: 'the government has decided ...'. But they know that getting to that outcome needed a lot of hard bargaining, compromises, deals and an eye to future interaction over other issues, i.e. they recognize the structured interaction. They are also likely to recognize (though less likely to talk about it) that the scope both for decision and for negotiation is framed and limited by widely shared understandings and values. Thirty years ago, policy action on climate change would scarcely have been contemplated; but since then, a succession of international conferences has focused attention on the issue, the body of scientific knowledge has been expanded and publicized, the stances of political parties have shifted, and people have become more aware of the significance of their own practices in producing collectively experienced outcomes.

We can see the complex way in which these dimensions interact by looking at the familiar 'policy technology' of the public inquiry: faced with an uncertain or contentious policy issue, the government may appoint one or more distinguished figures to inquire into the issue, to receive submissions from the public, and to make recommendations to the government. On the face of it, this is an exercise in authoritative choice: the government wants to deal with the problem, and seeks advice on the best way for it to do so. Often, however, the issue is one on which organized interests have strong views, and an important reason for setting up the inquiry might have been to provide a location where these views could be aired and the search made for a mutually acceptable outcome: that is, the inquiry can be understood in terms of structured interaction. But the inquiry is also a venue for raising issues, trying out scenarios, extending the range of possible actions, and admitting new voices to the discussion: it is part of the social construction of the policy issue. But these three accounts are not mutually exclusive: if you were to ask the minister for which of these reasons the inquiry was set up, she might say 'all of them': effective policy development may call for specific actions by government, for greater interaction between stakeholders, and for broader public understanding of the problem and the possible responses.

We can think of these multiple accounts as recognizing different dimensions of policy practice, the 'vertical' (where the dominant account is authoritative choice), the 'horizontal' (where the dominant account is structured interaction), and the 'scene-setting' dimension, where the dominant account is social construction. Figure 3.1 attempts to show this diagrammatically – think of it as two axes crossing inside an apple, perhaps.

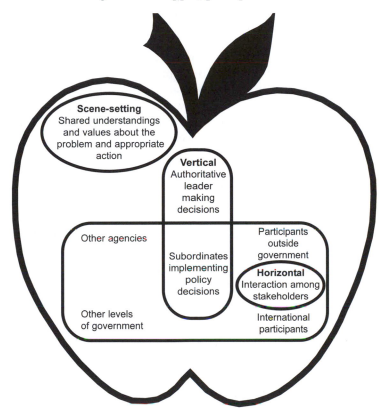

Figure 3.1 The dimensions of policy practice

These dimensions are not alternatives: rather, each tends to assume the others. The implementation of the authorized decision calls for the cooperation of relevant others outside the line of hierarchical authority. And shared understandings reached on the horizontal plane must be given effect via the instruments of the vertical dimension: the ministerial decision, the policy directive, the regulation. Policy practitioners use both accounts: they recognize the need to try to ensure that the relevant interests have been involved in framing the policy outcome (horizontal) before it is presented for official approval (vertical). In their more reflective moments, they are likely to recognize also that there is another dimension, where their contribution is less direct: the sphere of shared understandings and values within which the negotiation and the decision-making take place; we can call this the scene-setting dimension, and it would be described in terms of the social construction account.

This is taking us away from the 'common-sense' perception of policy-making as being about decisions by leaders. There are a number of people involved, in different ways, and it may not help to try to distinguish between 'policy-makers' and 'policy-takers'. Certainly, there are people in positions of visible authority – the minister, the commissioner, the secretary – and they are clearly important elements in the process. Policy authority may be seen as resting in some collective body at the top of the system, and the question is how policy business gets to this body. It may be that the cabinet makes policy about education, for instance, but it would be extremely rare for the cabinet to make a policy decision on education other than on the recommendation of the minister for education. Normally, the cabinet's role in the making of policy would be to accept the minister's recommendation, or, less commonly, not to accept it, in which case the minister has to go away and try again. The minister's initiative would usually have originated with specialist officials further down the line.

However, to say that the role of the cabinet (or the minister or director-general or secretary or commissioner) in policy-making is to accept or reject the recommendations of specialists does not mean that it (or they) is not 'really' making policy (with the implication that the 'real' policy-makers are the people who draft the recommendations). The policy process involves mobilizing authority (e.g. of the cabinet) in support of the programmes of officials; and, while it is possible to divide the participants into 'real' policy-makers and subordinates (or into 'real' policy-makers and well-publicized rubber stamps), this may not sharpen the accuracy of our analysis.

The point here (and this keeps cropping up in the study of policy) is that terms such as 'policy-making' are not neutral, technical terms: they are also part of the resources of the participants. The officials want to get the cabinet's endorsement of their plans in order to strengthen their hand in dealings with other interests. For this reason, they want to emphasize the cabinet's role. It may be that the proposal was approved by cabinet on the basis of a one-minute presentation by the minister which no one was interested in discussing, but the outcome will be presented as 'the cabinet has decided . . .'.

Rather than dividing the policy world into 'policy-makers' (who have authority and make decisions) and others (who haven't and don't), we should see 'authority' as a construct which frames the world in particular ways, and gives particular sorts of standing to people to participate in the policy process. It means that ministers are there as of right, whereas the others have to establish their right to be there, and to do this in ways which defer to the standing of ministers. The specialists are there to advise their minister, and experts from outside the bureaucracy have to find a minister to whom they can direct their advice. The specialists' plans are couched as submissions for the approval of the ministers, who are seen as having a moral pre-eminence on the strength of their authority. 'In the end,' it is said, 'the minister must have the last word.'

But who has the first word? Putting it like this raises questions about what happened before the issue came to the attention of authority figures like the minister. We would probably find that the issue had been around for some time, and a number of people and organizations had been involved. The notion of authority gives these participants a particular standing in the game: the minister has the last word (which may mean that the minister does not come into the story until people are ready for the last word); the education department, as the main advisers to the minister, has a central role in managing the process; the faculty of education at the local university may be called in but has no right to be there; various sorts of organized interests may seek to have their say; and unorganized individuals (such as the parents at the local school) will probably have no place at all. This does not tell us how likely it is that particular people will participate, or how significant they will be, but it does help to understand the relationship between the formal presentation of policy as authorized decision-making, and the experience of the participants.

We should also note that the flow may run both ways: from the top down and from the bottom up. Authority figures such as ministers may be trying to pass directions down the line, but lower-level participants may be trying to pass business up the line, seeking authoritative endorsement for their plans. In order to do this, they have to relate to the structure of authority: schools wanting action on some policy issue would probably press their case through the education department, where they are 'insiders'. But parents wanting action would be more likely to seek out the central parent organization as a body which has the authority to speak for parents. An immigrant family, however, with no social networks and limited English, would probably find it very difficult to use either of these channels to make their voice heard on a policy matter.

Accounts and links between the participants

Policy-making, then, is generally a collective process rather than an exercise in individual heroism. We can, in many cases, see the emergence of what might be called 'policy collectivities': relatively stable aggregations of people from a range of organizations who find themselves thrown together on a continuing basis to address policy problems. These people, whom Davies (1994: 3) describes as 'camped permanently around each source of problems', may or may not be formally recognized, but they can play a very significant part in the policy process.

Often, the linkages among the participants are formally recognized. The interdependence of functionally organized officials – e.g. between health, welfare and housing – is fairly obvious and can result in several different sorts of official response. One is the creation of formal links between these agencies, such as inter-departmental committees. These bodies, either ad hoc or permanent, offer a way for these agencies to cooperate with one another. They also offer scope for them to resist one another: if the agencies see themselves as being in a competitive struggle with one another, the dynamics of inter-agency bodies is likely to be 'Politics between Departments' (Painter and Carey 1979).

The other common official response is to establish a consultative body which will include not only the functional officials but also participants from other governmental bodies and from outside government, e.g. from business, community organizations and the universities. These bodies give a opportunity for participants from a diversity of organizations to discover the extent to which they can support one another. They also help to constitute the thing for which they are called into being: the Barley Industry Advisory Council is a major force in getting farmers, traders, processors, association officials and bureaucrats to see themselves as part of something called 'the barley industry', and to think in terms of policy for the industry. These bodies are less likely than the inter-departmental committee (which finds it difficult to escape from the continuing internal struggle for resources) to produce a negative, defensive reaction. Policy officials in government may seek to identify a single voice to speak for the clients or beneficiaries of the policy – for instance, the formation of a single farmers' association to speak for farmers – because it is easier for government to deal with organized interests than with unorganized ones, and it is worth providing a subsidy to, for instance, a national consumer organ-ization so that there can be a single voice to speak for this very diffuse interest.

Drawing the interested parties into the policy process in this way tends to make them 'insiders'; does it make others 'outsiders', and what determines whether outsiders as well as insiders can partici-pate in the process? Coleman and Skogstad (1990) identified two tiers within the policy community: a 'sub-government', mainly of officials, who dominated the process, and an 'attentive public', the participants who had an interest in the policy question but who did not have the same standing, might give the question less of their attention, and would not carry the same weight as the members of the policy community.

The extent to which 'outsiders' can become involved is a matter of degree: most policy issues would call for some degree of 'outside' input, whether of other officials or of non-officials. But there are degrees of 'permeability'. In some areas, policy is an 'inside job': policy matters are the concern of the agency with responsibility for the area, and there are no other significant participants with an interest in taking part in the policy process or the capacity to do so. In these cases, the place to look for policy formation is the agency – not only what it says, but also what it does, how it is organized, and the matters to which it pays attention – and to some extent, the political leaders who preside over it. More commonly, the policy area is of concern outside the agency, but mostly to specialists, and it does not attract a great deal of public attention. This facilitates the development of links among these specialists. Such links may be more or less stable, and to the extent that they are, we can identify a 'policy collectivity', identified in the literature by such terms as 'policy community', 'issue network', 'sub-government', etc.

Policy collectivities do not have to be formally recognized to be significant, and even where they are, not all of the relevant participants may have been included on the formal body. But there may be a shared awareness among the participants of who the relevant people are in their line of business, even if there is no formal body to which they all belong. Moreover, outside observers may see the stability and pattern in the process even if the participants are not conscious of them. Observers of the policy process have used a variety of labels to identify them, and these labels tend to highlight different aspects of the process. Some convey images of power. One of the earliest labels applied to a policy collectivity was 'the iron triangle', which was a term from the Vietnam War applied as a metaphor for the way policy was made in regulated industries in the United States. There, it was argued, policy was not made by the President or the regulatory body which he had appointed, but emerged in the interaction between the regulatory agency, the industry association, and the relevant congressional committee. The term conveyed both the strength of the policy collectivity and the relative weakness of the regulatory body when acting on its own. This metaphor was extended by the term 'sub-government', which admitted a wider range of participants into the policy collectivity, but again presented it in power terms: it is the group that governs.

Other labels focus on linkage, and, specifically, on the way that making links forms networks. Some writers object to talking about the policy collectivity as whole (e.g. to using the term 'community') because, they say, it does not operate as a whole; rather, when something comes up, people make links with relevant others. The network that is formed in this way, they argue, cannot be thought of as an organization: participants know the people near them in the network, but do not act in terms of the network as a whole. Furthermore, networks are very specific: the network which emerges over school buses might be quite different from the one that forms over school discipline, so rather than talking about a 'policy network' in relation to schools, we might identify a number of 'issue networks'.

The most common image of the policy collectivity has been that of community. This suggests intimacy and trust: policy is made among people who know and trust one another. This does not mean that there cannot (as in any other community) be ignorance, misunderstanding and conflict. Community, though, is an image which stresses the extent to which stable collective action is linked to mutual understanding: there needs to be some mutual understanding to have any collective action, and the practice of working together reinforces this understanding.

This image also draws our attention to the knowledge that policy collectivities share. They are drawn together by their shared awareness of a particular policy area. In some cases, this may be a new way of understanding the world, as happened with the emergence of environmental policy. For this reason, researchers studying the way policy in relation to global warming was made have talked about the emergence of an 'epistemic community', i.e. a group of people who understood what was meant by global warming and why it was a problem. This does not mean that they would all agree on what should be done about it, but they did not have to persuade one another that something needed to be done.

Using multiple accounts

It is useful for analytical purposes to distinguish among power, linkage and community as elements of the policy collectivity, but these are not mutually incompatible, and there is no reason why more than one element should not be present in any particular case. Coleman and Skogstad (1990) argue that a policy community has two elements: a 'sub-government' and an 'attentive public' – or, in terms of this analysis, a power-focused centre and an epistemic community on the periphery. Sabatier and Jenkins-Smith (1993) argue on the basis of a number of cases that a policy community contains two 'advocacy coalitions' in competition with one another, i.e. that there are epistemic communities being mobilized in the contest for power.

It is important to remember that these terms are essentially metaphors, introduced to help us make sense of the complexity of the policy process. They focus our attention in particular ways. In particular, they direct our attention to the social and interactive dimensions of the policy process, as distinct from the linear and hierarchical perspective which underlies much discussion about policy-making. But they should not be seen as definitive and mutually exclusive categories, and they do not in themselves make things happen in the way that things actually do happen.

Expanding our focus from 'who makes policy?' to 'who

participates in the policy process?' gives us a more complete picture, but it is important not to assume that participation is a game in which anyone can and does play. In the first place, not all those with an interest in a policy question will necessarily have a place at the table, and even if they do, not all seats are the same. Those concerned may have to establish their right to participate, and some writers distinguish between 'insiders' (who will be involved) and 'outsiders' (who would like to be), or between, as we have noted, a 'sub-government' of insiders and an 'attentive public' outside. Those who represent a challenge to the existing policy may be seen as 'disruptive' and are likely to be marginalized.

This can be very important, because who participates in a policy issue helps to shape what the issue is. As we saw, different participants are likely to have different perspectives on the question. Doctors are likely to see drunkenness as a question of personal health care, social workers to be concerned with its impact on relationships and the household budget, whereas the police are likely to see it as a question of public order. To the extent that doctors have a dominant voice in the discussion, the policy problem will be defined in health terms; to the extent that drunkenness is seen as a health issue, doctors and other health professionals will be seen as the appropriate people to discuss it (the relevant participants). Social workers and the police might constitute both the policy question and the relevant participants differently. In this sense, the problem and the participants are 'mutually constitutive': the one reinforces the other. Neither who the 'decision-makers' are, nor the problem they are addressing, is self-evident: they are constituted in the policy process.

Who is counted as a policy participant depends on which account is being used. In the authoritative choice account, attention focuses on authority figures – ministers, chief executives, boards of directors, national executives, etc. – and the people and processes that surround them. This appears more straightforward in government organizations, where 'policy' tends to appear in the organization chart: policy branch, policy officer, etc. In business and non-governmental organizations, the term 'policy' is less common. Non-governmental bodies tend to use different terms to refer to processes which in government would be called policy. They might speak instead of mission statements, corporate goals, strategic planning, or positioning.

This helps to explain why much of the mainstream literature

identifies the source of policy as 'the government'. Policy is 'whatever governments choose to do or not to do' (Dye 1985: 1). Policy seems to be the major concern of the highest levels of government, and the work of the executive – i.e. such figures as the prime minister, the president and the members of the cabinet – seems to be dominated by the taking of policy decisions. In Westminster systems there is an elaborate procedure for framing policy proposals which filter up the bureaucratic hierarchy, receive the approval of the minister, are discussed with other departments, and finally go before the cabinet. Once they are approved there, all the ministers are committed to support them and they become 'government policy'. Other forms of government, or intergovernmental bodies like the European Union, have their own procedures, but they share the assumption that policy is enunciated, or at least approved, by the people at the top.

In a structured interaction account, it would not be assumed that these public and prestigious figures are driving the policy process. Their policy role is usually a consequence of their place in the political leadership game, and they tend to serve in a range of positions, for relatively short periods – perhaps two to three years. They are presiding over large bureaucracies of whose work they may have little prior knowledge. There has been an enormous amount of discussion in the literature about the relationship between political leaders and expert officials. The political leaders will probably have ideas of their own about the direction in which they want policy to go, but the officials will have more ideas, more specific ideas, and more sense of which ideas will work. And they will be closely involved with the organized bodies with an interest in this area, who in turn will have ideas and initiatives to urge on the government. So the driving force for policy is more likely to be the institutionalized body of expertise over which the leader presides.

What is regarded as expertise, and how different sorts of expertise are related to one another in the policy process, reflect the climate of opinion both among policy professionals and in the wider public arenas – this is the social construction of policy. The social construction account sees that environmental policy emerged as a major policy concern in the West in the second half of the twentieth century. This was not because factories had suddenly become polluting, but rather because the campaigns of environmental activists had made the factories' contribution to pollution no longer acceptable to the public. (See Crenson (1971) for a classic study of this aspect of policy.) And as we noted above, Al Gore is clearly a policy participant – and perhaps a more significant one than President Bush.

So we can see that we need to use all three accounts to get a complete perspective on the policy process. For instance, take the development of policy on smoking. The requirement for cigarette packets to contain health warnings was imposed by government decision (authoritative choice), though it usually came as a result of intense struggle between health authorities, anti-smoking lobbyists, cigarette manufacturers and the advertising industry (structured interaction). Restrictions on smoking in government offices might also be seen as policy through authoritative choice. Similar restrictions in private offices, imposed by companies wishing to create non-smoking workplaces, gave rise to an industry norm. Although this might not be regarded as policy in the authoritative choice account, it would be in the structured interaction and social construction accounts (and in any case, company action was in many cases followed by occupational health and safety regulation to require non-smoking workplaces, putting it back on the authoritative choice account). So the question of what is regarded as 'policy on smoking' depends on how we are using these three accounts.

The point here is that, usually, all involved would be concerned that any initiatives were seen as the work of the political leadership (i.e. use the authoritative choice account). When Australian Airlines, for reasons of its own, sought government action to prohibit smoking on its flights, it was anxious not to be seen to be responsible for this, and sought to deflect responsibility onto 'government policy'. Similarly, the work of specialist tribunals is seen as being concerned with the implementation of policy, but to a large extent the policy is what they implement. To have a policy that puts restraints on free trade should not be allowed unless those restraints are in the public interest; and to set up a tribunal to decide if they are, means that the tribunal's interpretation of what is in the public interest becomes the substance of the policy. However, the wording used protects the presentation of the policy process: the contribution of officials is described as 'policy advice', that of stakeholders as 'consultation', and the work of the tribunal as 'interpretation'. So the dynamics of the policy process tend to privilege one account of policy (authoritative choice) over the alternatives.

'Policy-making', then, takes place in different ways and in

different locations, and the language used tends to shape the perception of policy. The authoritative choice account concentrates our attention on a point of decision; the structured interaction account spreads it to ask who can participate and how they get there; and the social construction account asks how situations are regarded as normal or problematic, and whose voices are heard. It is convenient to think of policy in terms of explicit official statements (authoritative choice), but this overlooks factors which may be equally significant but less obvious: the organizational dynamic of government and the activities of affected groups (structured interaction), the shaping of discourse about the subject, and the players' quest for recognition as serious participants (social construction). Benson identifies three levels: an 'administrative surface level' of official agencies, an 'interest structure' of networks and organized interests, and the 'rules of structure formation' which govern the policy agenda (see Ham and Hill 1984). In the authoritative choice account, policy is made when the authorized decision-maker gives assent, so attention is focused on the ministerial office, the cabinet room, the parliament. When the structured interaction and social construction accounts are admitted, it becomes harder to identify a point at which policy is 'made'; rather, we see a continuous process of framing and reframing.

> The public policy process is then a multi-person drama going on in several arenas, some of them likely to be complex large-scale organizational situations. Decisions are the outcome of the drama, not a voluntary willed, individual, interstitial action. Drama is continuous. Decisions are convenient labels given post hoc to the mythical precedents of the apparent outcomes of uncertain conflicts.
>
> (Schaffer 1977: 148)

Nevertheless, the authoritative choice account maintains its dominance because of the way in which it structures the action and facilitates the acceptance of outcomes. In this sense, it is a 'good account', but not because it is an accurate description of the process. It is important that we remain aware of the existence of these divergent accounts and identify the way in which they are used in the policy process.

Further reading

The authoritative choice account of policy as the product of decision-making has tended to be taken for granted by those using it,
and it has been investigated largely by its critics. The classic critique
is Lindblom's (1959, 1979), although Stone (1997), Jones (1994),
Jones and Baumgartner (2005), Jones *et al.* (2006) and Griggs
(2007) are all worth reading. Other writers pointed to the collective
nature of policy development; Haas's (1992a) discussion of epistemic communities is particularly interesting, and useful discussions
of the extensive literature on types of policy collectivities (policy
communities, issue networks, sub-governments, etc.) can be found
in Kenis and Schneider (1991), Börzel (1998), Dowding (1995, 2001)
and Miller and Demir (2006). The discussion on insiders and outsiders among policy participants is also interesting: see Maloney *et
al.* (1994) and Dudley and Richardson (1998). Haas's (1992a, b)
work on the knowledge base of policy collectivities links structured
interaction to the social construction account. Two useful studies of
the social construction of particular policy concern are Gusfield's
(1981) study of drink-driving and Nelson's (1984) study of child
abuse. The subject is also helpfully discussed in Roe (1994), Yanow
(1996) and Hajer and Wagenaar (2003).

4

What Is It For?

Cross-examining the obvious: policy as the systematic pursuit of goals

The question 'what is policy for?' is not often asked, perhaps because the answer seems obvious. Both participants and observers are comfortable seeing it as the exercise of authority to achieve collective purposes: policy is the pursuit of goals. The assumption that policy is a purposive course of action (Anderson *et al.* 1984: 4) underlies the mainstream definitions of policy. Lasswell and Kaplan (1970: 71) define policy as 'a projected program of goals, values and practices', Bridgman and Davis (2000: 6) define policy as 'a course of action by government designed to achieve certain results', and Friedrich (1963: 70) puts it bluntly: 'It is essential for the policy concept that there be a goal, objective or purpose.'

The policy process is then represented as a sequence of stages in the development and pursuit of this goal, beginning with thought, moving through action and ending with the solution. These stages are often presented not as a line, but as a circle, suggesting that there is a natural progression from one stage to the next. Figure 4.1 shows the 'stage' or 'cycle' model of the policy process.

In this perspective, the policy process is seen as a number of successive stages:

1   *Determining goals.* Authorized leaders determine the objectives they wish to achieve.
2   *Choosing courses of action.* They then select the courses of action which will realize these goals, preferably from a range of options, and in the light of the relative costs and benefits of each.

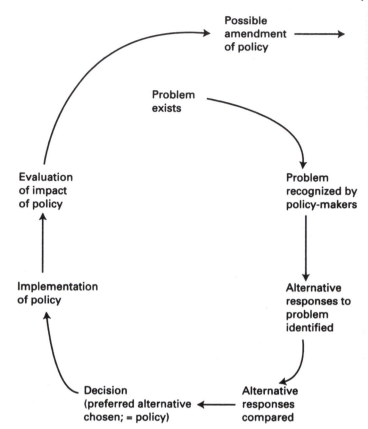

Figure 4.1 The 'stage' or 'cycle' model of the policy process

3   *Implementing these courses of action.* Other workers then have
     to carry out the courses of action that have been chosen, and
     the rest of the organizational process is described as the
     implementation of these choices.
4   *Evaluating the results.* The outcome of the implementation of
     the decision can (and should) now be evaluated. Was the
     decision thoroughly and economically put into effect (efficiency
     evaluation)? Did the implementation of the decision have the
     expected impact on the problem to which the policy decision
     was addressed (effectiveness evaluation)?
5   *Modifying the policy.* If necessary, the policy is then amended in
     the light of the evaluation.

Policy as choosing goals

To see policy as choosing and achieving goals appeals to common sense because it rests on some widely held assumptions: first, that we are ourselves rational, utility-maximizing individuals; secondly, that all organizations are set up to pursue goals; and thirdly, that, for governments, these goals are to improve, in some way, the welfare of individuals.

This assumes that government is a single entity, with a mind of its own: coherent, instrumental and hierarchical. It exists to carry out purposes, and these are defined at the top. It may receive advice from other organizations, but does not need the approval of any other body. On this perspective, policy is the specification of these purposes, and it is implemented when the purposes are achieved.

The assumption that government is there to maximize the welfare of individuals comes from Jeremy Bentham, the nineteenth-century Utilitarian thinker, who held that the justification for government lay in its capacity to advance the greatest happiness of the greatest number. This approach, extended by the concept of Pareto optimality (the best action is that which makes someone better off and no one worse off) has been at the base of mainstream policy analysis (see Jenkins-Smith 1990: ch.1). Much attention has been devoted to finding ways to calculate the 'best' policy option, generally based on a calculation of the relative advantage to different interests of the achievement of the desired goal of each of the options.

This focus on the selection of goals seems to be consistent with the practices of the higher levels of government, which are focused on identifiable choice-points ('decisions'), so that policy workers spend a lot of time marshalling issues so that they can be processed into decisions. They prepare 'submissions' for consideration by a political leader (minister, secretary) or group of leaders (cabinet, legislature). These are formal proposals which lead from an exposition of the problem to be addressed through possible responses to either a recommended course of action or some options. When the leaders approve this proposal, it becomes their decision and is implemented by officials. (Conversely, the practices of officials are seen as the implementation of some previous decision.) In this way, the leaders are said to be determining the overarching goals, and thus to be making policy. But to what extent can this be seen as the choice of objectives for action?

- These decision points (e.g. cabinet meetings) are focused on present practice as much as on ultimate objectives – e.g. the allocation of available funds among competing claimants. Up to a point, this might show the relative weight that these leaders give to particular policy concerns (though it might also show the relative political strength of the various leaders in the argument). Only in a very limited sense ('to give more money to welfare') could this be regarded as an objective.
- Where goals can be identified, they are often vague and ambiguous, and offer little guidance for action.
- There are often multiple goals, which overlap and frequently contradict one another. For example, 'the goals of our immigration policy are to protect our cultural integrity, to promote family links, to facilitate the migration of labour, to protect the employment of the existing workforce, and to meet our international obligations'. These are all valid statements of the desired outcome, but it is likely that pursuing one would be at the expense of another, so to describe the action as the pursuit of these policy objectives does not take us very far.
- Where there are multiple goals which conflict with one another in this way, the outcome is likely to be a compromise which reflects the power of different interests, inside and outside government, and which is not an objective of any of the participants, but a situation which had to be accepted in order to get a decision (and which all of the participants might seek to overturn).
- In many cases, processes of goal selection seem to have greater symbolic value than substantive impact.

Policy as the implementation of goals

In the goal-oriented perspective, policy is about both choosing goals and achieving them. The policy embodies a theory of cause and effect: if we do *a*, then *b* will result. When the policy-makers' intentions have been carried out, the desired objective should have been achieved: this is 'implementation'. But if what we find on the ground is significantly different from these goals, then the policy has not been implemented. This was the perspective taken in the pioneering book on this subject, Pressman and Wildavsky's *Implementation*, first published in 1973. They asked, 'why was it that the goals articulated by the policy-makers in Washington bore little relation to what could be seen on the ground in Oakland, California?' When the question was put like this, it was immediately and widely recognized to be a general problem: in all policy fields, there was a 'problem of implementation', in that the outcome was likely to be quite different from the originally stated intentions. Therefore it was not simply a matter of determining the policy goals: they had to be put into effect.

Pressman and Wildavsky explained the lack of implementation in the Oakland case in terms of the large number of participants in the process, and the diversity of goals. Most of the things to be done needed to be 'cleared' at a number of points, involving a range of participants with distinct perspectives of their own and different levels of commitment to the policy objectives. The more the policy depended on such 'clearances', the more likely it was that the original objectives would not be accomplished.

This was also reported in other studies of implementation, which found a number of other causes for policies not being implemented: the original decision was ambiguous; the policy directive conflicted with other policies; the policy was not seen as high priority; there were insufficient resources to carry it out; it provoked conflict with other significant players; the target group proved hard to reach; the things that were done did not have the expected impact. Over time, circumstances changed, and attention shifted to other problems, which made the original goals less important. Indeed, the literature is a little depressing because it seems to be largely about 'implementation failure'.

Whether implementation is a problem, and what sort of problem it is, depend on the account of policy that we are using. In the authoritative choice account, implementation means that authorized decisions at the top coincide exactly with outcomes at the bottom: did 'the government' achieve its objectives? This reflects constitutional models of government and instrumental models of organization: it is seen as self-evident that 'those elected by the public to government should be able to place their policies into action' (Linder and Peters 1987: 465). This is the account which generated the problem: since the process of government often did not result in outcomes which coincided with clear prior goals, there must be 'a problem of implementation'.

However, in the studies of 'the problem of implementation', the focus has been not so much on the goals as on the process and the people through which these goals would have to be pursued, and it becomes clear that many of the participants are not so much trying to 'implement' the programme in question as trying to do their jobs, and they are interested in the programme to the extent that it can contribute to their own agendas. Constructing the programme is an exercise in generating commitment among the participants whose support is necessary, which means that the final shape of the programme reflects the concerns of the stakeholders who have come on board. For instance, in addressing unemployment among young people, political leaders may be anxious to be seen to be taking action, but are uncertain about what would be the best thing to do, and are hearing different views from the different stakeholders. Welfare and labour market agencies are concerned to find ways to manage the growing pool of young unemployed. Employer groups complain about the low skill levels and motivation of job applicants, criticize the school system, and call for trainee programmes with lower pay and less job security than regular employment. Vocational training institutions push for an expansion of training programmes, but unions are suspicious that traineeships may be used as cheap labour and threaten the position of skilled workers. The finance department, which is concerned with controlling spending, may see the proposal as a fresh and potentially expanding spending commitment. What is finally endorsed by the political leaders, and the shape it takes on the ground, will reflect the different agendas of these stakeholders. In this account, the question about implementation is not so much 'did the government get what it wanted?', because there was no clear goal to start with, but more 'what emerged from the interaction of the various stakeholders, and how did it relate to the concerns originally expressed?' on this perspective, the initial authoritative statement is only one part of the process, not a definition of the only acceptable outcome.

In this process of structured interaction there would be argument about the nature of the youth unemployment problem, its causes, and what might be appropriate responses to it. In what sense is unemployment problematic? Do some young people see it as normal? Is unemployment the result of 'skill deficits' in the unemployed, or does it reflect global economic change (e.g. manufacturing moving from the industrial West to Asia)? If there are skill deficits, are these the result of rigidities in training and labour market institutions (e.g. focusing on manufacturing as the economy shifts to services) or of changes in the labour market itself (e.g. the increasing use of casual and part-time labour)? It might be that a plan to build more technical colleges does not get support because stakeholders feel that if the existing structure of job training has not produced an appropriately skilled workforce, and the least skilled are the most alienated from these institutions, 'more of the same' is unlikely to change the situation, and better ways of reaching the inadequately skilled, with more use of IT, are called for. In this social construction perspective, though, this would be described not as a failure of implementation but as a modest achievement in rethinking the problem.

Recognizing that 'implementation' may also be about interpretation and negotiation poses a difficulty for implementation as a concept: what is it that is being implemented? In the authoritative choice account, 'policy' emerges fully formed from the head of the 'policy-maker'; in the structured interaction account, it is something which emerges from the interaction among the relevant participants; in the social construction account, underlying all of this negotiation there are competing accounts of what causes the problem and what can be done about it. It is not that the policy was complete when it first emerged and was then at risk in the interaction that followed, but rather that it was this collective process of interpretation and negotiation which produced the proposal which was agreed to by the leaders – i.e. 'the policy'. This changes the question about implementation from the execution of a clear objective, to the achievement of collective action which is compatible with the perspectives of all the relevant participants.

It also recognizes the time dimension, i.e. that the process does not begin with a detached 'policy-maker' articulating a new policy and inscribing it on a blank sheet, but that it is part of a continuing game in which a regular cast of participants recognize and respond to policy questions. The game is not fixed – new players seek to be recognized, and there is contest over how policy questions are to be understood – but there is continuity as well as change, and policy initiatives have to take their place in this ongoing process, leading Sabatier (1986) to suggest that the timeframe for the implementation of a new policy should be ten or twenty years.

Implementation, then, is a concept in use, framing the policy process in terms of the formal definition of objectives and the collective pursuit of these objectives. This is not a good guide to the process, but it is a good way of validating it, and a basis for critique. For the analyst of the policy process, though, the question is not so much 'did the programme get implemented?', as 'how did the creation of a programme reflect the contribution of the various stakeholders, and what impact did it have on practice?'

Evaluation and goals

In the 'policy cycle' model, evaluation completes the cycle: it enables policy-makers to know to what extent they are achieving their objectives, and to act accordingly. The common sense of evaluation is clear: if policy is concerned with achieving goals, then it is only sensible to check whether or not these have been attained. In the words of one manager, 'My objective is to see evaluation used to improve the design and performance of government programs, my ultimate goal being *demonstrably effective programs*' (Wholey 1981: 92).

It has become increasingly common for evaluation to be built into the policy process, particularly as part of the relationship between institutions: legislators may demand that the activities of officials are evaluated, control agencies (such as finance departments) may demand evaluation of operating agencies (such as departments of agriculture or education), and central governments may attach evaluation requirements to grants to regional or local governments or non-governmental bodies. Who can object to a systematic check on whether policy objectives are being attained?

An elaborate methodology of evaluation has emerged, incorporating the policy objectives, the hypotheses about change and ways of measuring outcomes. For instance, if the policy problem is seen as the high death toll among young drivers, a policy of incorporating driver training in the school curriculum might be instituted (i.e. the source of the problem is seen as low skill levels, which can be addressed by the training programme). The evaluation might measure the death toll among trained drivers after the programme was instituted, monitor a comparable group of untrained drivers and compare the death toll among trained and untrained drivers, using measures of statistical significance. From this, the evaluators could form conclusions about the impact of training on the death toll, and the policy-makers could act on the basis of these conclusions, i.e. if it were found that the death toll among trained drivers was no different from that among untrained drivers, then the training programme would be cancelled.

We may well find, though, that there is a demand for driving training in schools despite the evidence that it does not appear to make any significant difference to the death toll. It may be that the training is supported by school principals because it is a good way of keeping year 10 occupied while their exams are being marked, by parents because they are always happy for the schools to do systematically things which they would otherwise have to do themselves, and by motoring interests because it smoothes the way for young people to become car owners. Consequently, any attempt to close down the programme would be met with strong opposition.

To the extent that the policy process is seen as goal-oriented, it makes sense to measure progress towards these goals systematically. But if there is divergence over goals, agreement has to be forged at a more superficial level: we can agree more readily on what to do than on why to do it. What the driver training example suggests is not that people are pursuing shared goals, but that there is a variety of values (not necessarily shared, but not inherently inconsistent with one another) that can be mobilized to support a particular programme. However, not all reasons are equal, particularly in public; we can identify 'sacred' accounts which all will subscribe to in public, and 'profane' accounts which the participants will use (and be guided by) in private (see Colebatch and Degeling 1986). 'Improves the driving skills of young people and saves lives' is a 'sacred' presentation, and commands wider support than 'gets the children out of our hair while we mark the exams' or 'prepares the next generation of car buyers': these are 'profane' presentations. The 'sacred' presentation – its impact on the death toll – supports claims on resources and is used by all advocates.

For the participants, this divergence between the presentation of policy as the pursuit of goals and the experience of the policy process is disconcerting. One response is that there is always a gap between the real and the ideal, and the goal presentation is an ideal to which everyone subscribes but which will never be completely achieved. By contrast, Guba and Lincoln (1989) argue that we need to move from a goal-oriented, compliance-focused approach to evaluation, to a process-oriented, development-focused approach (which they call fourth-generation evaluation), in which the evaluator is not an outsider bent on control, but an insider striving for improvement, a quality assurance adviser rather than an inspector. In a way, this is an argument for a shift from an authoritative choice account to a combination of the structured interaction and

social construction accounts; certainly, it is an argument that evaluation has to be seen as part of an ongoing process, not as a
normative judgment.

Alternatives to goals

The presentation of organized activity as the pursuit of defined
purposes has a slightly unreal character to it. It is not that statements of purpose cannot be found, or do not command assent, it is
that there seem to be a number of other processes at work. People
in organizations want to show their professional skills, execute the
standard operating procedures of the organization and maintain
stable relations with the organization's clientele. In doing this, they
may well refer back to statements of purpose, which clearly have
some significance, but it would be misleading to see their activities
simply as attempts to achieve these purposes.

Policy is also about *routine*: 'the department's policy on late
essays is . . .' means 'this is the routine which we have adopted for
dealing with this situation'. This is easy to parody as the emergence
of bureaucratic procedures which have no relation to (in this case,
educational) goals, but all organization is about routinization –
developing known and predictable ways of dealing with events.
Organizations develop standard operating procedures, and these
are likely to be different in different organizations. Allison (1971)
points out that the differences between the standard operating
procedures of the Pentagon, the CIA and the State Department are
critical to an understanding of the American policy process during
the Cuban missile crisis. They had different ways of acquiring,
processing and evaluating information, and came up with quite
distinct understandings about what was happening and about what
response was appropriate. Policy practitioners may well recognize
two different types of policy: explicit rationales and purposes as one
type, and the recognized regularities in the organizational process –
the standard operating procedures – as the other. They may also
amend their own practice in recognition of these differences among
organizations in understanding the problem, e.g. by holding joint
(inter-agency) planning meetings.

This is why the evaluation of organizational activity does not
simply ask whether goals were achieved. The work of a school-
teacher, for instance, might be evaluated in terms of the students'
achievement of the defined learning objectives, but it is likely that

there will also be a more mundane way of evaluating it: Are there any disciplinary problems? Is the level of classroom noise within normal expectations? Are there any complaints from parents? Do the pupils progress to the next grade without difficulty? This 'process-oriented' way of evaluating the work of the organization may run alongside more formal 'objective-oriented' exercises in evaluation. Education inspectors, school principals and parents are likely to have different ways of evaluating what goes on in the classroom. By extension, we could say that they have different educational objectives, but this would require us to translate their perspectives on process into clear objectives, and this may be rather artificial. It would not surprise us to find that the school principals prefer classrooms to be quiet, disciplinary problems to be few and parents to be uncomplaining, but does this mean that these are their objectives for the school?

Looking at it in another way, we can see that policy is also about *structure*. Organized activity is shaped not only by the proclaimed goals but also by the nature of the organizational forms through which it happens. For instance, the policy that a high school parents' and citizens' association might adopt to orient students to the workplace is likely to look rather different from the equivalent policy pursued by the education department. The local parents' and citizens' association is likely to operate in a more individual way, tapping known individuals and working through personal contacts, whereas the education department, which has to deal with a range of schools and knows little about their links with the workplace, is likely to operate more formally, to define standard procedures and to seek out central organizations of employers with whom to negotiate. In this context, the key questions are not 'what do we want to achieve?', but 'who takes responsibility for this?' and 'what resources – staff, money, the attention of those higher up – can they call on to do it?'

So because policy is, as we noted, 'a structured commitment of important resources', reformers often seek changes not only to the formally stated goals of the organization but also to the structure. Environmentalists may demand that the road-building agency not only adopt a policy goal of protecting wildlife habitats, but also set up a habitat protection unit in the agency, staffed by biologists, and may demand that all large construction projects be accompanied by an environmental impact statement which makes specific reference to habitat.

Sense-making and action

March and Olsen argue that observation of the organizational process does not suggest that organizations are best understood as means to achieve clearly understood goals:

> Information is gathered, policy alternatives are defined, and cost–benefit analyses are pursued, but they seem more intended to reassure observers of the appropriateness of actions being taken than to influence the actions. Potential participants seem to care as much for the right to participate as for the fact of participation; participants recall features of the process more easily and vividly than they do its outcomes; heated argument leads to decision without concern about its implementation; information relevant to a decision is requested but not considered; authority is demanded but not exercised.
>
> (March and Olsen 1989: 48)

Instrumental analyses of organization, they argue, validate action better than they explain it (March and Olsen 1989: 25). When participants in the policy process mobilize the dominant paradigm of instrumental rationality to make sense of the action in which they are engaged, that paradigm frames the action in a way which makes that action both comprehensible and legitimate, offering a framework which enables people and values to be appropriately located and recognized.

Policy participants find that, much of the time, they are concerned not so much with transmitting instructions within an organizational hierarchy as with negotiating with people outside it – people who share an interest in the policy question but have a distinct perspective on it, and whose cooperation cannot be taken for granted. In this context, there is a good deal of ambiguity about objectives: can they be identified?, how consistent are they with one another?, and to what extent do they help us to make sense of the action? Policy workers are involved in developing and maintaining networks through which the various participants can relate their shared concerns to one another, and the discourse through which they can do this. And this calls for the use of different accounts at different times. The authoritative choice account gives legitimacy: for example, officials in the environmental protection agency can seek more staff in order to implement the goals announced by the government and enforce the statutes passed by the legislature. And structured interaction and social construction give efficacy: the officials know that in order to secure the change in practice which the official goal envisages, they will need to get the cooperation of industry organizations, regional government bodies, the standards authority, environmental groups, their own inspectors in the field, and others. To get this cooperation, they will need to have a base of shared understanding about the situation, the appropriate responses, and the responsibilities of the various participants. But it may be that producing a quick response for the minister (authoritative choice) will alienate industry bodies whose cooperation is sought (structured interaction), and that the rapidly drafted official announcement (authoritative choice) means quite different things to the various participants (social construction), and does not reflect a commitment to an agreed pattern of action.

This means that the participants will be using different accounts at different times. The participants may find that the structured interaction and social construction accounts make sense of their own experience, but that the authoritative choice account is better for making sense of it in public: it has normative force, because it shows the outcome to have been reached in a valid way. It is important that public presentation of the outcome is expressed in the authoritative choice account – e.g. 'the minister has decided …' – even if the decision was the result of an agreement between officials and representatives of the affected interests, and the minister showed no interest and signed the final document without reading beyond the first page. Empirically, it may be that it is a decision of those affected, to which the minister has assented, but normatively, it is the minister's decision.

So participants have different accounts of the same process available to them. One account is *sacred*: it draws on the normative framework, and talks of the rational pursuit of legitimately chosen objectives: 'the policy objective is …' The other account is *profane*: it draws on the empirical framework, and talks about contest between agencies, about process and ambiguity (see Colebatch and Degeling 1986). Participants recognize that which account is used depends on the circumstances: when making a speech to parliament, the minister would be likely to use the normative account ('the government has decided …'), but this would be out of place in a planning meeting of officials. Journalists make stories out of the contrast between the normative and the empirical accounts ('What *really* happened?').

Mobilizing goals in action

The goal orientation is also mobilized to create *order*. It is not that there *is* a clear and shared purpose underlying policy, but that participants accept it as proper that there *should* be. This means that they may confront the fact of the existence of different perspectives on the nature of the activity and what it is that is valued through a discourse about goals. Yanow (1996) relates that at the annual planning meeting of a public organization in Israel, the director would ask the meeting, 'What are our objectives?' Her first thoughts were, 'Doesn't he know?', but it was clear that this was a way of inviting participants to engage with the organization by expressing their various perspectives in a comparable way. Such an invitation may produce a quite diverse set of goals. For instance, the goals for a forestry agency might include:

- 'to maximize the contribution of forestry to the economy';
- 'to derive the optimal sustainable yield from the forests';
- 'to sustain the livelihood of logging communities';
- 'to maintain the forests as a habitat for flora and fauna'.

Expressing the different perspectives in terms of a goal makes it easier to deal with the fact of their diversity. The worth of each perspective has been recognized, and attention is directed to how to frame action in a way which recognizes the different perspectives. This is often done by trying to draft a set of goals to which all the participants can give assent, e.g. 'to derive the optimal return from the community's forest resources while maintaining the natural ecosystems'. Such statements tend to be very broad, and are sometimes dismissed as almost meaningless – 'motherhood statements' – because while all the participants may assent to them, they do not give a clear guide to what will be done. But their meaning lies in the fact that they do exist, and that participants from all the diverse policy perspectives can draw on them (in different ways) for support. In this way, goals provide a framework for the negotiation of order in the policy process.

There is a link, then, between statements of goals and the exercise of control in organizations, but it works both ways. It is not simply that leaders in organizations seek control in order to accomplish purposes: people also articulate purposes as a demonstration of their claims of leadership. Would-be political leaders, in particular, are asked 'what is your policy on x, y or z?', but in a range of organizational contexts, leadership is demonstrated by articulating purposes. This is part of the 'cultural construction' of leadership in organizations, i.e. it is what people expect leaders to do (and sometimes, something that leaders would rather avoid doing because they realize how difficult it is to meet all the expectations).

The goal orientation is also important in negotiating relationships outside the organization. For instance, the justice agency might adopt a juvenile crime prevention policy, aiming to reduce the incidence of crime among young people, and seeking the cooperation not only of the courts, police and welfare agencies, but also of non-governmental organizations and the school system. These other bodies might have little interest in the incidence of juvenile crime – e.g. the schools are likely to see their role as being to educate children, and not to be a general agency of social control – but articulating a goal to which few could object becomes a way of trying to mobilize support from a wide range of sources. Just as statements of goal can be used to create common ground within the organization, so they can do the same across organizations.

This illustrates the way in which the language is itself part of the action. While talk of 'the government's overall objectives' might seem empirically unrealistic, given that the members of the government spend most of their energy pursuing their individual agendas, and generally come together only to struggle over scarce resources, having the concept of overall objectives enables them to conduct this struggle indirectly, as a struggle over symbolic statements, e.g. whether the objectives talk about 'growth' or 'equity' or 'sustainability' or 'competitiveness'. The words are broad, but the differences between them are significant, and the participants are trying to mobilize language in a way that supports their own perspective.

Policy workers have to operate with all these ambiguities. They know that the public presentation of any policy must invoke authoritative choice. But they also know that authorization is rarely enough, and that to be effective, authoritative statements need to be backed by interaction aimed at incorporating the 'significant others' into the final outcome, and generating a shared understanding of which the authoritative statement is the official expression.

Further reading

The perception that policy consists of the pursuit of known goals is deeply rooted in the 'common-sense' understanding of the world, and tends to be assumed, rather than analysed, in the policy literature, and even those authors who do not share it tend not to ask why it is so widely used. Jenkins-Smith (1990) has a good discussion of this 'utilitarian assumption', and Sabatier and Jenkins-Smith (1993) argue that the dynamic of policy is coherence around values rather than the pursuit of agreed goals. March and Olsen (1989: ch.3) offer a useful critique of the instrumental assumption, and Kingdon's (1984) discussion of agenda-setting and Edelman's (1988) analysis of the symbolic aspects of the political process are also valuable correctives. The main alternative to the instrumental assumption is the interpretive approach, which we discuss further in Chapter 6, but Fischer (2003) gives a good overview. Yanow's *How Does a Policy Mean?* (1996) is a very perceptive analysis of the interplay of authority, organized interaction and meaning formation in the policy process. Sanderson (2002) is a very helpful review of the claims for 'evidence-based policy' as part of a rhetoric of instrumentality.

It is also instructive to follow the way in which the idea of policy goals is handled in Pressman and Wildavsky's pioneering study *Implementation*. The first edition, published in 1973, is framed in the authoritative choice perspective; as the well-known subtitle put it, it is about 'how great expectations in Washington are dashed in Oakland ...'), but in the second (1979) and third (1983) editions, the analysis focuses more on interaction and the construction of meaning.

5

What Else Is There?

We can see from the discussion so far that 'policy' is a handle on the way we are governed, a concept which we use to make sense of what we see and what we do. But there are other, closely related concepts which are also in use, and it may sharpen our understanding of policy to examine these other terms, to ask what aspect of governing they refer to, and how they relate to policy. In this chapter, we select eight key concepts for closer examination: politics, administration, management, organization, structure, regulation, governance and governmentality.

Policy and politics

One reader of an earlier edition of this book suggested that a discussion of the distinction between policy and politics should come much earlier in the book 'as it is central to policy-making practice'. In this case, it is surprising that the distinction does not exist in the major European languages. The exception is Dutch, which uses *beleid* for policy and *politiek* for politics, but *Politik* in German and *politique* in French cover both the English words, and it proved quite difficult to translate 'policy-makers' into Italian (Ostrom and Sabetti 1975: 41). 'Politics', 'policy', 'polity' and 'police' are all derived from *polis*, the city-state of ancient Greece, and when the word 'policy' first emerged in English, it tended to refer to the whole pattern of governing, as in Sir Thomas Smith's *The Manner of Government or Policie of the Realm of England* (*c.* 1565). But, over time, distinct usages evolved, and as a German political scientist noted, 'policy' came to acquire in English a 'noninstitutional, purely intentional sort of meaning', and to be further distinguished from 'politics' (Heidenheimer 1986: 4). Why this happened is not clear, but the 'state tradition' in England came to focus on the centrality of the elected legislature, and 'policy' came to be used in relation to competition between the parliamentary parties and, in particular, to electoral platforms: policy was what the politicians wanted to do. In this presentation, the legislators determine the direction of government: that is, they decide 'policy'. In the process, they struggle with one another, and appeal for support – from the voters, from fellow legislators, and from outside interests: this is 'politics'. The permanent officials of the civil service are to abstain from any part in this struggle, and then implement the policies of the winners in the legislature. This is, clearly, an authoritative choice account: the elected leaders make the policy, and the officials carry it out.

This formulation served to explain and to justify the place of representatives and officials in the process; whether it was a good description was another matter. If politics is seen as a contest over the right to make policy, clearly, one will impact on the other. But since there were two terms, distinctive connotations have developed: for instance, that policy is concerned with outcomes, whereas politics is concerned with process – and, in particular, with the participants' position in the game. Policy is seen as detached, but politics is partisan, e.g. doing favours for supporters. The demands of the struggle for advantage ('politics') might be at odds with the pursuit of a desired goal ('policy'). For instance, putting off action on a contentious issue might be 'good politics but bad policy' (Prasser 2006).

But while we can distinguish between the connotations attached to 'policy' and 'politics', it is difficult to separate them in practice. We recognized that part of the structured interaction account of policy was the contest between participants. Even though many of the participants are seen as agents of the government, they have their own distinct perspective on the process, and they are (to a greater or lesser extent) in continuing competition with one another – for resources, for the attention of the leaders, and for influence. This means that questions like 'who are the people proposing this?', 'Do they think like us and tend to support what we do?', or 'Will we need their support in the future?', will always be relevant.

So there is always an element of politics in the policy process, but the distinction between politics and policy is drawn on in shaping the action. Special staff may be appointed to ministerial offices to do 'political' work (i.e. related to the struggle for partisan advantage) which is deemed inappropriate for permanent officials. It may be, for instance, that the task of mobilizing support in the legislature for a change in agricultural policy has to be given to the 'political' staff, but that it is acceptable for permanent officials to be engaged in mobilizing support among industry groups. The two terms carry different connotations, and there is a strong normative element in the distinction, with 'politics' tending to come off second-best in the comparison.

Policy and administration

The distinction between policy and politics is balanced, in a sense, by the distinction between policy and administration: politics is seen as what leads up to policy-making, and administration as what flows from it. In this view, the policy process has two stages: first, decisions are taken about the goals to be pursued ('policy') and then people give effect to these decisions ('administration'). This analytical distinction between types of activity is equated with a division of labour among the participants: there are some people whose work is to choose goals ('policy-makers') and others whose work is to give effect to already-determined goals ('administrators'). In the American literature, it is often the members of the legislature who are seen as the 'policy-makers'. In Westminister-type systems, the policy-makers are assumed to be the ministers, and perhaps the most senior officials as well.

Distinguishing 'administration' from 'policy' in this way reinforces the place of legitimate authority, because it is the people in authority who are seen to determine the goals, and officials simply determine how best to accomplish them. Organizations are instruments for the accomplishment of authorized purposes. This presentation of the action also insulates officials from the involvement of the leaders in the detail work of government: their role is simply to determine the goals; it is for the officials to find the best way to achieve them. This was the primary concern of reformers like Woodrow Wilson, the professor of public administration who went on to become president of the United States, who asserted the need to make this clear distinction, and to buttress it with a permanent and non-partisan civil service, in order to get good government: efficient and impartial administration is the implied counterpart of authorized policy (Wilson 1887).

The attraction of this analysis is that it is easy to grasp and it explains a number of things: not only where policy comes from, but also why participants are in the game, and what they do. But as an empirical statement, the explanation looks a little forced. Administration consists of more than simply responding to the choices of authorized leaders. It seems inadequate to say that the officials who are running the public schools or the agricultural extension service or the immigration agency are simply giving effect to the prior decisions of ministers or legislators. They are specialists with a commitment to their area of activity, who from time to time need to get the support of these authority figures, but they are not dependent on them for goals. Nor should we assume that all the activity of officials can be explained as the pursuit of some authorized goal. Empirical observation suggests that these participants are also responding to pressures from their clientele, collecting information, using their specialist skills, and generally keeping the show on the road. In other words, 'administration' cannot in practice be seen as a separate and subordinate sphere of action: we find 'politicians performing administrative duties and administrators assuming political responsibilities' (Caiden 1982: 82). The separation of the two is described as a 'myth' (Hughes 1994: 35).

Why is there this gap between the model and what we see around us? A common explanation is that there has been a shift in practice: once, there was a clear distinction between policy and administration, but in contemporary conditions, this is no longer the case (see Hughes 1994). Or the model may be described as an 'ideal' which is normatively desirable but not attained in practice.

A different explanatory approach is to take the myth seriously, that is, to see it as 'a narrative created and believed by a group of people which diverts attention from a puzzling part of their reality' (Yanow 1996: 191). The presentation of public action in terms of authorized decision and administration to give effect to it answers the problem of where direction comes from in government, and how it may be changed: it comes from the electoral process, and the subordination of officials to authorized representatives: this is 'administration'. This is an account of government which is open to empirical challenge, but as Cuthbertson (1975: 157) says, a myth is 'immune to factual attack'. So the account is enunciated by participants on public occasions as part of the sacred, and recycled in academic accounts, but immediately belittled as a historical survival or an unattainable ideal, whereas in fact it is neither, but is a way of making sense of the governmental process in specific contexts.

Policy and management

In the past twenty years, the term 'management' has been used much more in contexts where 'policy' might have been used. Gunn (1987: 33) argues that, in the 1950s, the dominant concern in the study of the public sector was with institutional reform and the term used was 'public administration'. In the 1960s, there was a new interest in planning – 'rationalist exercises in strategic decision-making' – which were associated with the term 'public policy'. In the 1980s, the concern was to reduce public expenditure and to adopt the methods of the private sector, and the term 'public management' became more common.

In some ways, this is an extension of 'administration': authorized leaders determine the goals, and public managers carry them out. In other ways, it suggests a move away from the subordination of the policy/administration split: 'management' implies more autonomy, more scope for initiative.

Some see this change in the terminology as reflecting a substantial change in practice. Hughes, for instance, argues that there has been 'a transformation in the public sectors of advanced countries' which has made the traditional distinction between 'policy' and 'administration' obsolete. Whereas 'public servants carry out policies derived from others ... Instead of merely following instructions, a public manager focuses on achieving results and taking responsibility for doing so' (Hughes 1994: 1, 5-6). He cites Allison's (1971) exposition of the functions of general management: 'strategy' (establishing objectives and devising plans to achieve them), 'managing internal components' (meaning your own staff), and 'managing external constituencies' (other parts of your organization, other organizations, the press and the public), and argues that these functions are now 'routinely carried out by public servants' (Hughes 1994: 62). In this context, 'policy' becomes redundant. Hughes sees 'public policy' as meaning 'policy analysis' and as being 'mainly concerned with the application of formal mathematical methods in the public sector' (p. 145).

The increasing use of 'management' to describe the steering of public business can be traced back to the reform agenda of the 1960s and 1970s, when it tended to complement the concern for 'policy': there should be a focus on the desired outcomes ('policy') and goal-oriented managers should then be commissioned to achieve them. This was succeeded by the 'reinventing government' rhetoric of the 1990s (see Osborne and Gaebler 1992), which argued that public officials should be given the autonomy to find innovative answers to public problems, and that they should be 'steering, not rowing', that is, seeing that services are delivered, but not necessarily delivering them themselves.

The 'new public management' also put the focus on managers, but usually in conjunction with a neo-liberal agenda which was rather suspicious of government. The main principles of the new public management have been summarized by Foster and Plowden (1996: 45–6) as:

- separating the purchasing of public services from production;
- serving consumers rather than bureaucratic, political or producer interests;
- using market prices rather than taxes;
- where subsidizing, doing this directly and transparently;
- extending competition;
- decentralizing provision;
- empowering communities to provide services;
- setting looser objectives, and controlling outputs rather than inputs;
- bringing about deregulation;
- preventing problems through planning rather than curing them afterwards.

In some ways, this reinforces the goal-orientation – by arguing that authoritative leaders should determine goals and then contract with agencies to deliver them – but in other ways, it gives the managers more autonomy and discretion about how these goals are to be achieved. This could mean different things in different places, as managers work out different ways to pursue these goals; therefore, what policy actually means would be subject to local negotiation.

The new public management approach was grounded in 'public choice' theory, which sees public officials and public organizations as being driven by self-interest. The task of steering is therefore less about where we want to go and more about how to induce other people (who are all self-interested) to cooperate. It puts stress on the use of market competition: if leaders specify the outcome to be achieved, they can then contract with one or more competing suppliers to deliver it. These suppliers might be in the public bureaucracy, in commercial firms or in community organizations. The task for the public manager is to ensure that the specified outcome has been delivered. On the other hand, there is a theme of empowering both managers and clients, and it is not always clear why the deals that autonomous managers and empowered communities might conclude would necessarily be preferable to hierarchically imposed policies.

There is also the question whether discussions of new public management describe what is or has been achieved or whether they advocate what could be or should be. Much of the writing does not distinguish clearly between empirical and normative accounts of the world: Hughes's suggestion that 'traditional' public servants had no goals of their own but simply followed instructions from their ministers, would not get a great deal of support from ex-ministers. But to the extent that the analysis of the new public management is descriptive, it recognizes that public officials are not simply the passive recipients of authorized directions, which was noted in the policy literature in the debate over top-down and bottom-up perspectives. It also recognizes that relations have to be conducted with external constituencies, which is what we have been discussing in the structured interaction account of policy.

Policy and organizational process

What we are seeing here is that policy is concerned with the process of organizing public authority: 'policy', 'politics' and 'management' are all labels for ways of steering public organization, each making its own assumptions about the dynamics of public organization. This organizational dimension is often not specifically addressed in the writing about policy, except perhaps as a source of imperfection after the event, e.g. the 'problem of implementation'. But the study of policy has been grounded in perceptions of the way organizations work (particularly, but not exclusively, in the public sector), and the gap between the way they do work and the way they should.

This can be seen in the long-running debate over 'rational' versus 'incremental' decision-making. The debate can be traced back to an article by Charles Lindblom in which he criticized the idea of decision-making as a comprehensive search for the optimal route to the achievement of known ends (Lindblom 1959). Lindblom argued that, in practice, means and ends are not separable, analysis is limited rather than comprehensive, policy emerges from a succession of small changes rather than a single clear decision, and the test of a good decision is not so much that it achieves known objectives, as that people agree with the process by which it was reached. But, he argued, this method (to which the name 'muddling through' was attached) was as rational and systematic as that based on clearly specified objectives.

This provided the base for a set-piece encounter in policy texts and courses between 'rational' and 'incremental' decision-making, but this did not seem to help either the analysis or the practice of policy. Indeed, it was claimed that the mainstream position was that whereas the rational model showed how decisions ought to be taken (i.e. was a normative model), the incremental model best described the actual practice of decision-making in governments (i.e. was an empirical model) (Howlett and Ramesh 1995: 137).

Lindblom's argument was framed in behavioural terms but he was making an organizational point, noting that the argument for comprehensive rationality assumed that the decision-maker was in some way outside the action, inscribing decisions on a tabula rasa – a clean sheet – with no limitations implied by existing activities. In fact, the decision-makers are part of the action, starting from some position, and confronting the fact of the activities of other people. They tend to begin with the assumption that what they are doing is worth doing, and to the extent that they contemplate alternatives, to think of ones that are rather like what they are doing now. Where changes are sought, they tend to be ones which will meet with acceptance from the other participants rather than opposition. Lindblom argued that the rational choice approach assumed a single decision-maker, but that in fact there were many participants, each with diverse perspectives and interests, and limited ability to force the others to accept their position, so that the outcome was reached by a process of mutual accommodation – 'partisan mutual adjustment' – rather than by a single-minded choice.

Lindblom's critique was elaborated in a number of books and articles (see Lindblom 1959, 1965, 1979; Braybrooke and Lindblom 1963; Gregory 1989; Lindblom and Woodhouse 1993; Parsons 1995), and generated a great amount of debate. The debate was not helped by a confusion between analysis and advocacy (see Smith and May 1980), which led to Lindblom being criticized as an 'apologist for pluralism', but it was also hindered by the lack of interest in the organizational dimension. It did not, for instance, draw on the political science research into 'policy collectivities' (the structured interaction account of policy), or the implications of this perspective for the concept of a rational decision. So it is worth drawing attention to the two significant shifts in analytical focus that Lindblom was introducing into the debate:

- a shift from the desired outcome of policy to the process by which policy is made;
- a shift from the logic of the system as a whole to the logic of the participants.

Lindblom's contribution expands our focus on the policy process; so too does Graham Allison's study of policy-making during the Cuban Missile Crisis. In *Essence of Decision* (1971), Allison suggested that there were three distinct perspectives that could be used to understand US policy-making:

1 *The rational actor.* The action is between identifiable actors – in this case, 'the US' and 'the USSR' – which have clear goals and make choices about the best way to achieve these goals.
2 *The governmental process.* Policy is not made by 'the US' but emerges from the interaction of a range of specialized bodies – e.g. the Pentagon, the CIA, the State Department, the White House – each with its own distinct way of recognizing and dealing with problems.
3 *Bureaucratic politics.* These specialized bodies have different interests and positions, and the policy process is about power relationships between them.

Allison argues that it is not that there are three different sorts of policy-making: all of these elements are part of the total picture. The 'rational actor' is perhaps the most familiar: there always seems to be an implicit assumption that organizational action should be determined by rational choice. The policy task, then, is to clarify what the preferences are, to set up the policy question as a choice between alternatives, and to systematically evaluate the relative merits of the alternative ways of achieving these preferences.

The organizational process perspective is grounded in empirical observation: although people might talk of organizational goals, organizational activity seems to have more to do with process than with the pursuit and achievement of goals. It is more by specialized procedures than by outcomes, and, in this sense, by organizational inertia. This is not to suggest that the organization is doing nothing, but rather that it is doing what it has always done. Organizations operate through routines: new situations are analysed in terms of past practices. Each organization has standard operating procedures (SOPs) which its members understand and use, and Allison shows that in the Cuban Missile Crisis, the differences between the SOPs of the Pentagon, the State Department, the CIA, etc., made a big difference to the way the policy problem was addressed. The implication is that organizations do what they do because it is the appropriate thing to do in that situation, not necessarily in order to achieve some known outcome.

The bureaucratic politics perspective recognizes that it is not simply that the different participants have distinct views on the world: they are competitors – for resources, for attention, and for the right to frame the policy question. In order to build its new road, the highways agency must overcome any opposition from the environmental protection agency. There is a time dimension, too: the way they deal with one another on any given issue will reflect their experience of previous encounters and their expectations about the future. In order to advance their concerns, they will need to take note of where they stand in relation to the other participants in the policy process. They will be aware of the positions that other participants are likely to take, and will consider the possibilities of support, alliance and opposition. Even if they do not like the idea of 'playing politics', it will be in their interest to think strategically, otherwise they will simply be the consumers of the strategies of the other participants.

Allison stressed that these should not be seen as three different types of policy process, but three different lenses through which to view the one process. In any policy situation there will be elements of choice (rational actor) and routine (governmental process) and contest (bureaucratic politics), but they will not be the same for all the participants, or at all times, or in all policy fields. Using the three lenses gives us a sharper focus on any given instance of policy activity, whether it is being made or changed or just kept in place. Some sceptical political scientists argued that this was leaving out of the policy picture the question of interest. The central element in the governmental process, they argued, is constituent benefit: it is about getting benefits for your side. This analysis could be applied to organs as such (see Georgiou 1973; Aldrich *et al.* 1994), but is largely applied to 'public politics', and is perhaps best exemplified by Lasswell's (1936) classic text *Politics: Who Gets What, When and How*.

Policy and structure

The title of Lasswell's book also reminds us that policy is not about context-free decisions, but about continuing patterns of allocation – of resources, of rules and of attention. Some things are noticed and attended to; others are not. Typically, people who make their living from agriculture are supported through governmental agencies which run extension activities, marketing supports and subsidy schemes, and taxation rules give special consideration to the fluctuating incomes of farmers. But people who make their living from art have few such advantages: there is rarely a department of art, and certainly not one which can match the muscle and resources of the department of agriculture.

This is the argument for seeing policy as a structured commitment of important resources. That farmers are more favoured by the policy process than artists reflects not so much the goals of authoritative decision-makers as the strength of the institutions which support them – not only the organizations (though they have a strong organizational base in government) but also the discourses in use (e.g. 'industry support', 'price stabilization', which are applied to agriculture but not to art) and the underlying shared values (farmers are seen as more worthy of support than artists).

For this reason, policy reformers look for structural change as well as endorsements of goal – not only for statements of support for the environment, but also for the establishment of an environmental protection agency. Setting up the agency demonstrates the importance of environmental values, and because it provides a location where environmental issues are taken seriously, it becomes a focus of attention for environmental scientists and activists outside government. In this way, it structures policy. This is why Giddens (1984) argues that we have to think of structure not as a thing but as a process. He explores the relationship between structure and action, and concludes that they have to be seen as two elements of the one dynamic: that structure frames appropriate action, and that when people act appropriately, this re-creates the structure. He argues that this process (which he calls 'structuration') takes place in three ways: through the organizational forms in use ('structures of domination', as he puts it), through the discourses in use ('signification') and through the values which people hold ('legitimation').

Putting this into the policy context, it is clear that the policy of support for agriculture can be seen not only in the speeches and policy statements, but also in the organizational forms and shared values which lie behind them. Similarly, while there may be policy statements of support for art, they are not backed by strong organizational forms, inside or outside government, or by the deep-seated values which underlie the protection of agriculture. This also means that changing the policy of support for agriculture is not simply a matter of taking a decision, but calls for changes in the policy discourse, in the organizational forms, and, ultimately, in the way that agriculture is valued.

Policy and regulation

The process of governing is sometimes labelled 'regulation', a term which conveys a clear impression of control from above: the government regulates. In the United States, where public utilities are often provided by private companies which have monopoly rights, these companies are subject to the jurisdiction of independent regulatory bodies, and, for instance, the extent to which a power generator should take note of the environmental consequences of its activities may be seen as a matter for the regulatory body. There is an extensive American literature on how state power is or should be used to regulate in the public interest, and it is very much concerned with 'regulatory capture': how to ensure the independence of the regulator from the industry that it regulates. As regulation was enlarged to cover such matters as air pollution, there was a tendency for very specific criteria to be written into the legislation so that the regulator would not make 'sweetheart agreements' with industry.

There has been a renewed interest in regulation in Europe, first by neo-Marxists (see Boyer 1990), but then by both academics and practitioners as public authorities try to create a single European market, which involves drawing national regulatory structures into a common European framework. This has been an exercise in 'market-shaping', and while the predominant discourse has been about deregulation, it has really been just as much about re-regulation. Vos (1999) points out that the policy goal of having a single European market forced the European Commission to become involved in the detail of health and safety regulation. And while the new regulatory regime rests on the regulatory power of the EU (i.e. it can be seen as 'authoritative choice'), it has involved a great deal of negotiation with affected parties. This can be seen as 'regulation' or as 'policy' – Héritier (1999) calls it 'market-making policy'.

This perception of regulation as something created through negotiation rather than imposed from above has also been explored and expanded by researchers from such fields as law and economics, who point to the way in which the force of legal rules rests on the values and social practices of the people to be governed as well as on the words of the rule or the efficiency of the compliance mechanism. They point to the ordering of social practice through involvement and self-regulation in fields as diverse as medical practice, retail trade and environmental protection, and argue for 'responsive regulation' (Ayres and Braithwaite 1992) in which the people being regulated are co-producers of the regulatory framework, and often its implementers. This approach to regulation has much in common with what is called in the EU the 'open method of coordination', which leaves national governments scope to decide how they will introduce the policy and avoids the need for precise directives from the European Commission – i.e. there is a strong element of structured interaction (see Hodson and Maher 2001).

This discussion suggests that the idea of regulation has broadened from the simple imposition of hierarchical control to a perception of ordering in which the participation and perspectives of those being regulated play an important part in the construction and maintenance of the order, which parallels the development we have noted with the concept of policy, expanding from a single focus on authoritative choice to one which also takes in structured interaction and social construction.

Policy and governance

One response to this growing recognition of the complex and interactive nature of governing has been to look for a new term, and 'governance' has become a popular label – so popular, indeed, that it is used to label widely different things. 'Corporate governance' and the 'good governance' advocated by the World Bank, for instance, have little in common with Rhodes's (1997) argument that Britain has moved from 'government' to 'governance', and, for many writers, 'governance' is just another word for the governmental process. But there is a core of shared themes in the discussion about governance that are relevant to our discussion of policy. Stoker (1998) identifies the key elements of the governance perspective as follows:

- Governance refers to the way that governing is accomplished by a complex set of actors and institutions from within government and outside it.
- It recognizes the blurring of boundaries and responsibilities for dealing with problems, with more involvement of business and non-governmental organizations.
- It recognizes that the relationships between the various participants in governing are characterized by power dependence: that is, that no single participant can accomplish unilaterally what needs to be done, and that there needs to be collaboration between players with different sorts and levels of resources.
- Governance implies that governing is accomplished by autonomous self-governing networks of actors.
- It recognizes that governing has to be accomplished by means other than authoritative command.

The governance perspective, Stoker argues, offers a map to help us make sense of the changing world of government, drawing attention to changes, puzzles, dilemmas and concerns. From the policy point of view, governance is addressing a broader range of issues, but the discussion traverses many of the issues that we have encountered in our exploration of policy. It challenges the assumption of the authoritative choice account that the policy task is to choose the right objectives and the best way to carry them out, focusing attention on the development of structured interaction, though it does not recognize these as distinct accounts, but assumes that we are in the course of a transition from governing through authoritative choice to governing by interaction.

Policy and governmentality

'Governmentality' is a term not widely encountered in the policy literature, but it has much to contribute to our understanding of policy. It derives from the argument of the French social theorist Michel Foucault that the process of governing rests on a body of shared understandings, recognized expertise, ways of evaluating practice, and technologies of rule – the 'mentalities of governing'. The discussion of governmentality focuses on the ways in which governing becomes 'only sensible', because both the need and the response seem obvious, and people are made into 'governable subjects'. This directs our attention to questions such as:

- *Problematization*: what is normal?, what is considered deviant?, what needs to be remedied?, and who should act?
- *expertise*: what is accepted as valid knowledge for defining problems and identifying appropriate responses?
- *identity*: how are people identified, both as actors and as subjects for action?
- *technologies of rule*: what are the ways that have been developed to govern behaviour?
- *governing at a distance*: the ways in which 'the government' may preside over a process of governing which is accomplished through actors who are organizationally distant from, even separate from, the authority of government.

As an example, identifying 'alcohol consumption' as a policy problem is an exercise in problematization ('Why is this a problem?') and in the recognition of expertise ('What are the dimensions of the problem?, What sorts of response would be most appropriate?, Most effective?, Who has answers to these questions?'). It also raises questions of the identities which are seen as relevant, both of the person drinking (e.g. 'problem drinker') and of the people who might be part of the governing (e.g. bartenders, police, medical staff). It points to the significance of technologies for measuring alcohol consumption (portable breath-testing devices to replace crude assessments of speech and balance) and the question of how they should be used. (Should they simply be devices for the police to enforce compliance?, Should they be built into car design to prevent alcohol-affected drivers from starting the car?, Should hospital staff test accident victims for alcohol consumption?) What are the ways in which the consumption of alcohol is governed 'at a distance', through a range of authorities and cues and practices, rather than by government direction?

This approach offers a different perspective on governing and the place of policy in it. In a way, the literature on governance shifts the focus from authoritative choice to structured interaction, and the literature on governmentality shifts it to social construction. It changes the question from 'how do the policy-makers govern us?' to 'how do we govern ourselves?' Like the discussion on governance, it takes a broader canvas, but it has significant lessons for policy.

Making sense of governing

There is no cause for alarm because of the range of closely related concepts in use. People – both participants and observers – try to make sense of the world in which they are engaged. They look for system, and they operate with the analytical devices which seem appropriate. For instance, the traditional literature on regulation is grounded in law and economics and is seen as correcting 'failures' in an already existing market. But the European Union found that regulation was needed to bring the single European market into existence: they were 'shaping' the market rather than 'correcting' it, and political scientists saw it as an example of governance. The question is not 'which analytical perspective is correct?', but 'how much does each help us to make sense of the process of governing?'

The perspective we are taking here would be called by some 'post-positivist', 'postmodern' or 'post-structuralist'. We cannot go into this in detail, but what these terms suggest is that we are recognizing that there are multiple ways of mapping the world of social action, there may be more than one in play at any one time, and the question is not 'which is correct?', but 'how are they used?' In the course of this book, we have moved from seeing policy as a thing – 'the policy' – written down and with a clear objective – to seeing policy as a way of explaining and validating action, in which the idea of authoritative choice becomes part of the structuring of social action. But, as we have seen in this chapter, it is not the only way of doing this, and we need to be aware of the other ways, and of the significance of using one analytical approach rather than another.

Further reading

There has not been a great deal of writing on what distinguishes policy from the alternative labels. The 900-page *Oxford Handbook of Public Policy* (Goodin *et al.* 2006), for instance, does not discuss it at all; policy, it appears, is just there. So it is worth taking a look at Parsons's (1995: 16–29) account of the emergence of a distinct 'policy approach' in political science. Heidenheimer's discussion of the attempt to distinguish policy from politics (1986) raises some interesting questions. Woodrow Wilson's (1887) argument for a clear distinction between policy and administration is often cited but tends to be dismissed as outdated and unrealistic. The argument for focusing on 'management' is made by Hughes (1994), and Foster and Plowden (1996) give a critical review of the significance of the new public management for government in the UK. Allison's (1971) analysis of the Cuban Missile Crisis shows the utility of thinking of policy as an organizational process, with choice, routine and contest as alternative lenses for making sense of the action, and Giddens's (1984) analysis of the structuring of action has a lot to offer the analyst of policy. Kickert *et al.* (1997) provide an empirically and conceptually informed discussion of the implications of organizational complexity for public sector management. The term 'governance' has been used in such a diversity of ways that it has been called an 'empty signifier', but Stoker (1998) gives a useful account of the core meaning, and Pierre (2000) brings together a number of views on how this concept can be used to sharpen our analysis of the governmental process. Rose and Miller (1992) give a good introduction to the governmentality literature, and Dean (1995) presents an interesting application of the approach to a policy question.

6

What Do They Say About It?

Writing about policy

If you enter 'policy' into a search engine such as Google Scholar you will be presented with over 20 million items: there is a lot written on the subject. But these writings are likely to approach the subject in different ways, with different questions, and (not surprisingly) tend to produce different sorts of answers. There is some fuzziness about the subject matter itself: is it 'policy', 'public policy' or 'policy analysis'? If it is 'policy analysis', is it analysis of policy (implying a critical detachment) or analysis for policy (implying commitment and a positive input into the process)? There is no room in this book to explore all the avenues which have been opened in the quest to understand policy; what we can do is to set out the main approaches in the academic literature on policy, and also draw attention to some of the other themes in the social sciences which are not expressly focused on policy but which I find helpful in the analysis of policy.

This chapter, then, is a sort of street map of the academic literature on policy; it is a brief, personal perspective, and more extensive coverage of the literature can be found in Parsons's pioneering survey (Parsons 1995), and in three recent collections: Peters and Pierre (2006), Fischer *et al.* (2007) and Goodin *et al.* (2006). This chapter identifies three distinct approaches to writing about policy:

- systematic instrumentalism
- adjectival policy
- analytical approaches

and also identifies some other writing in the social sciences which is particularly helpful in the analysis of policy.

Systematic instrumentalism

Most of the writing on policy is located within a meta-narrative that could be called 'systematic instrumentalism', that is, it sees policy as a conscious, systematic way of pursuing some known purpose. The increasingly authoritative Wikipedia (2008) defines policy as 'a deliberate plan of action to guide decisions and achieve rational outcomes', and while few would claim that this is always a good description of policy practice, it structures the way that people talk about it. Within this approach, there are many distinct points of focus.

Policy sciences

We might begin with the way the academics labelled their own work. In the years following the Second World War, when governments (particularly in the United States) had significantly expanded their range of activities, and intellectuals had become more accustomed to applying their knowledge in governmental contexts, there was a renewed interest in the application of the social sciences to problems of governing, and Lasswell's 'The policy orientation' (1951) was an appeal for the development of a 'policy science' which would be (a) multidisciplinary, (b) problem-oriented and (c) explicitly normative – that is, it was aimed at producing 'better policy'. But while there has been an enormous amount of academic and applied interest in policy, that interest has led not to the development of a 'policy science', but rather to a struggle between political science and economics for the soul of 'policy studies'. It could be said that political science won on the campus, but economics won in the corridors of power. A methodology, grounded in microeconomics, emerged for evaluating particular policies, and this was referred to (particularly in the United States) as 'policy analysis'. But the development of this methodology proved frustrating for the academics, who complained that the practitioners did not make use of their analysis, and then had to confront the question of whether they were going to involve themselves in the strategy of getting their ideas adopted (see Bardach 1977, 2000). This raised questions about the tension between the explicit normative orientation of the 'policy sciences' aspiration and the traditional detachment of the academic, and the academic writing has tended to be an outsider's account of the policy process rather than an insider's contribution to it. But policy analysis has been institutionalized both as a field of study (witness various courses and journals) and as a field of practice (there are, for example, positions and units for 'policy analysts' or 'policy officers') (see Wildavsky 1979).

Public policy

The most common descriptor in policy studies – the book titles, the search keywords, the course titles – is 'public policy', classically defined as 'anything a government chooses to do or not to do' (Dye 1972: 2). Others add qualifications and refinements to this rather fundamentalist definition, but the focus is on 'what governments do'. Among the qualifications, though, are the multiplication of the subject. Jenkins (1978), for instance, describes policy as 'a set of interrelated decisions taken by a political actor *or group of actors* concerning the selection of goals and the means of achieving them' (p. 15, emphasis added); whether what happens in the group of actors can be described in terms of individual choice ('the selection of goals') is a problem which is rarely examined.

This approach focuses attention on specific acts. Policy is seen as coming in small, explicit packages: a school truancy policy, an automobile emissions control policy, a tax reform policy. For some American writers, a policy is a statute: a specific action by legislators. And each policy act has an object. Friedrich (1963: 79) stipulates that policy seeks 'to reach a goal or realize an objective or a purpose'; Anderson (1997: 9) notes that 'the purpose or goal of governmental actions may not always be easy to discern', but concludes that 'the idea that policy involves purposive behaviour seems a necessary part of its definition'.

This means translating the process of government into a pattern of goal-directed action. Since governments make policies which are then translated into action, where governments are acting, it must be because of a policy, and what governments do is 'public policy'. Hale (1988) points out that in the 1980s, many courses and texts previously called 'American Government' were relabelled 'public policy'. Anderson (1997: ix) explains that his text *Public Policymaking* refers to 'policymaking in the United States, especially at the national level'. Hale suggests that this helps to explain the expansive character of the definitions offered:

> One popular text on policymaking defines policy as 'whatever governments choose to do or not to do' (Dye 1985: 1). (This recalls Mark Twain's description of the River Platte: 'a mile wide and an inch deep'.) Other texts make similarly expansive claims. 'Policy refers both to intentions and to actual results' (Gordon 1978: 355). What, then, was our policy in Vietnam?
>
> (Hale 1988: 436)

Seeing policy as 'choice by governments' leads to a distinction between 'analysis for policy' (= working out the best choice) and 'analysis of policy' (= how the government made the choice it did).

The 'stage' model

Policy, then, is seen as a process of choice, a succession of stages which mirror a model of rational individual behaviour: thinking first, then doing, then checking.

> ... a policy cycle is likely to begin with issue identification, and then proceed through policy analysis, policy instruments, consultation, coordination, decision, implementation and evaluation.
>
> (Althaus *et al.* 2008: 37)

Even if this is an accurate model of individual behaviour (which is questionable), it is difficult to simply translate it into collective behaviour. If the policy process involves a number of participants with different perceptions and interests, who struggle with one another to win support for their own agendas, to what extent can the outcome be depicted as a collective process of thinking and choosing?

Describing the process as 'stages in a cycle' is persuasive because of its neatness. What is not clear is whether this is descriptive ('this is what policy is like') or normative ('this is what policy ought to be like'). Accounts of the 'policy cycle' are often accompanied by warnings that 'the public policy process is not nearly as tightly sequential or goal driven as the cycle model makes it appear' (Howlett and Ramesh 1995: 198), and Bridgman and Davis (former Cabinet Office officials) say that the cycle model is both descriptive and normative: '[it] is a guide designed to inject rigour [into the policy process] ... good policy should include the basic elements of the cycle' (Bridgman and Davis 2004: 22, 24). The 'policy cycle' model is part of what Stone (1988) calls the rationality project: '[the] mission of rescuing public policy from the irrationalities and indignities of politics' (p. 4). It projects reassurance that policy outcomes have been reached in an appropriate way (even if this does not stand up to closer scrutiny), and it can be mobilized by some participants (e.g. the Cabinet Office) as leverage against others (e.g. the operating agencies of government).

Policy design

The desire to mobilize the policy sciences to produce 'better policy' has led to a good deal of writing on 'policy design', both as a concept in itself (e.g. Dror's (1971) *Design for the Policy Sciences* and as applied in specific contexts (e.g. Tinbergen's (1958) *The Design of Development*). This literature assumed the existence of expert 'policy designers' and discussed (at a fairly general level) how they should go about designing policies which would be successful. Over time, there emerged a realization that perhaps this is not simply a matter of having the appropriate skills in the back office: there are many actors, they may define the problem in different ways, there may be disputes about the causal links between phenomena, and the process of formulating policy may in fact be an important part of the policy (see Hisschemöller *et al.* 2001). There was also the question of whether the 'policy designers' should be involved in the 'post-design' phase: persuading the 'decision-makers' to adopt their design, participating in its implementation, and evaluating the outcome (see Bobrow 2006). This has meant that, for many of the academic writers, the focus has shifted from the skills of the designer to how policy workers manage the interplay between actors: Bobrow (2006: 88) suggests that we can distinguish between an 'institutionalist' school of thought, which focuses on the rules of the game, and a 'deliberationist' school, which aims to 'get the discourse right'. But in specific contexts, the focus is more likely to be on content – designing the right answer – and Dror (2006) argues that the need is to train policy-makers in the 'crafting' of what he calls 'grand policies'.

But where the academics may be diffident, the practitioners are confident. The UK Cabinet Office, through its Policy Hub website and the National School of Government, has been promoting 'best practice' models of policy-making, such as its *Professional Policy*

Making for the Twenty-First Century (Cabinet Office 1999). In particular, these models argue for linkage and coordination between agencies ('joined-up government') (see Pollitt 2001) and for the use of evidence in both the formulation of policy ('evidence-based policy') and its implementation (see Davies *et al.* 2000; also Davies 2004; Tenbensel 2004).

Decision-making

At the outset, bringing the social sciences to bear on policy questions was seen as a form of 'decision support', feeding directly into the decision process. Policy analysts were seen as 'advising the Prince' (Wildavsky 1979), and it was thought that the social science knowledge would enable better decision-making. The Planning, Programming and Budgeting System (PPBS) which Robert Macnamara introduced into the US Department of Defense in the 1960s was seen as the exemplar of a social-science-informed decision tool. This early enthusiasm faded, with policy analysts complaining that the policy-makers did not listen and policy-makers complaining that what the analysts produced did not help them to make decisions; there is less mention in the literature now of 'decision support'. More is heard about the choice of instruments for government action. Hood (1983) identified the 'tools of government' by the mnemonic NATO: Nodality (being at the centre of things), Authority (being able to give directions), Treasure (being able to extract and allocate money) and Organization (having a bureaucratic structure through which its concerns can be transmitted and acted upon). Bemelmans-Videc *et al.* (1997) were more abrupt; for them, the instruments of policy were 'carrots, sticks and sermons'. Other writing has been concerned with finer distinctions within these categories, e.g. whether financial inducements are offered through grants, loans, subsidies, taxation or other means (Bardach 2000). It appears to be like a round of golf, with the government having to decide which is the right club to use on each occasion.

Post-decision: policy implementation and evaluation

In the 'systematic instrumentalist' perspective, policy culminates in implementation and is followed by evaluation. Both have given rise to a substantial literature, and it is convenient to think about these two terms together since they encounter the same puzzles. If policy is defined as being goal-directed, the obvious test of success is whether the goal has been achieved. In their influential book *Implementation*, Pressman and Wildavsky (1972) analysed a federal programme in California and argued that the goals as defined in Washington had not been achieved because the participants on the ground in California had their own agendas of concern, and were interested in how the federal programme could contribute to these. Pressman and Wildavsky argued that this case illustrated the difficulty of securing the proper implementation of policy goals. Their argument sparked an immediate response, with many scholars writing about 'implementation problems', and it was elaborated by Sabatier and Mazmanian (1979), who set out a long list of conditions, which were required for policy implementation.

But the more attention that the question received, the more this simple model was questioned. Lipsky (1976, 1979) found that 'street-level bureaucrats' were not simply implementing the plans of others, but shaped policy as they worked out how to do their jobs; and Barrett and Fudge (1981) argued that the policy–action relationship is a continuing interaction, not a mechanical execution of clear programmes of action. Wildavsky modified his analysis too. In the second edition (Pressman and Wildavsky 1979) Giandomenico Majone joined him as a co-author, and they wrote about 'implementation as evolution', suggesting that policies did not emerge fully formed at the outset, but developed in response to the pressures and stimuli brought to bear, which meant that what was carried out might be rather different from what had been originally envisaged. By the third edition (1983), chapters had been added on 'implementation as mutual adaptation' and 'implementation as exploration', co-authored by Angela May Browne, and it was conceded that in this evolutionary framework 'it becomes difficult to assume the prior existence of objectives against which to assess accomplishment' (Pressman and Wildavsky 1983: 204). In recent years, less has been heard about implementation as a policy issue and, by 1997, Hill asked rhetorically whether it had become 'yesterday's question' (Hill 1997). His answer was no, and a book (Hill and Hupe 2002) followed which gives an extensive review of the writing on implementation and argues for its continuing importance.

In the same way, those writing on the evaluation of policy usually began with the assumption that the policy goals were clear, and the main task was one of specification and measurement (see Rossi and

Freeman 1993). Evaluation became a normal part of grant-aided programmes in the United States, and foreign aid generally, and the literature expanded. But it became clear that evaluation was part of the power relationship, and that defining just what it was that the programme was meant to achieve was not necessarily straightforward, either at the outset or once the programme was running (see Palumbo 1987). Evaluation was seen as a process of negotiation, and there were questions about the place of 'stakeholders' in the evaluation. Guba and Lincoln (1989) argued for a 'fourth-generation' evaluation which would be 'responsive' and not simply a top-down inspection. But at the same time, the moves to a more loosely structured public sector, with more contract-like relationships, spurred demands for 'performance indicators' across a wide range of public sector activities (see Jackson 1988). But 'evaluation' remained more salient than 'implementation', and the UK's *Professional Policy Making* document recognized the tension between judgement and development in evaluative practice (Cabinet Office 1999). Vedung (2006) tracks the research on evaluation, and Bovens *et al.* (2006) review the broader political questions surrounding policy evaluation.

Adjectival policy

Much of the writing about policy is addressed to particular areas of policy concern – health policy, environmental policy, immigration policy – and this writing has been labelled 'adjectival policy'. This writing could also be included under 'systematic instrumentalism', since it shares the assumption that policy is about authoritative choices to achieve known objectives, but the interest tends to be in the objectives rather than the process. It is characterized by an expert knowledge of the field and the history of government programmes, and many of the writers move between practitioner and academic positions. It is analysis for policy as well as of policy, following Lasswell's (1951) call for a policy science that is inter-disciplinary, problem-oriented and explicitly normative. There is a great deal of writing about each of these identified policy fields, but the different literatures tend not to have much to say to each other: they are directed to their field of practice more than to policy as a subject. The English publisher Edward Elgar has a series of reviews of adjectival policy; see, for instance, Bjorkman and Altenstetter (1998) on health policy, Marshall and Peters (1999) on education

policy, and Grant and Peters (2000) on agricultural policy. Peters
and Pierre devote nearly half their *Handbook of Public Policy* (2006:
167–394) to these 'substantive policy areas'.

Analytical approaches

The writing that we have surveyed so far can be seen as a com-
mentary on, and a contribution to, policy seen as an instrument for
the accomplishment of some common purpose. It has not been all
(or wholly) analysis for policy, but it has been located in a framework of systematic instrumental action. But much of the academic
writing on policy is less concerned with achieving the desired outcome than with understanding the process, and this sort of writing
we have labelled 'analytical' (which is not to deny that much of the
instrumental writing could also claim to be analytical).

Methodological questions

A major concern of the social science interest in policy has been the
development of appropriate methods for analysis. The first wave of
policy analysts in the United States came from economics and
operations research (Radin 2000), and standard US courses in
policy analysis assume a grounding in microeconomics and quantitative method (see Weimer and Vining 2004). When researchers
who were not applying quantitative methods also become involved
in policy research, debates about the worth of quantitative versus
non-quantitative ('qualitative') methods became inevitable. The
debates were inconclusive, but they did provoke researchers to be
explicit about their methods, and, in particular, stimulated the
'qualitative' researchers to show why their research could be considered as reliable and credible as the number-crunching of their
quantitative counterparts (see Sadonik 2006; Yanow 2006; also
Yang 2006). But some argued that the methodological canons of
academic social science were not appropriate guides to practice in
the 'real world' of policy work, where a 'quick and dirty' estimate
might be all that is possible in the circumstances, and advocated a
basic, 'practical' approach to methodological questions (e.g. Patton
and Sawicki 1993).

Rationality and action

For most writers, policy implies a more 'rational' approach to governing, with a more explicit link between goals and practice, and this assumption is explored in a number of ways in the literature. As we saw, the advocates of the 'stage' model (or 'policy cycle') saw it as the 'rational' approach to policy, which they contrasted with the 'incrementalist' approach of writers like Lindblom, although many (analysts and policy practitioners) would argue that incrementalist behaviour is usually the most rational course of action. But some writers have subjected to closer scrutiny the whole idea of what constitutes rational behaviour in the complex policy world, which is not made up of single actors with firm preferences and a clear idea of how to realize them, but is characterized by divergent values, overlapping games, ambiguous goals and multiple timeframes (see Andrews 2006; Jones *et al.* 2006).

The term 'rational' is also applied to an interpretation of government known as public choice theory (also called rational choice or rational actor theory), which 'takes the tools of economics, and applies them to the materials of politics' (McLean 1987: 1). It offers a map of social action populated by calculative and self-regarding individuals, who always act so as to maximize their own benefit. Government is not an independent force serving collective interests, but a prize for self-interested redistribution. Politicians are entrepreneurs offering promises of reward in exchange for votes; bureaucrats are driven neither by policy nor by expertise, but by the desire to maximize the size of their agency; voters sell their votes to the politician offering the best (and most credible) promise of reward. From these premisses, public choice theory develops logically consistent scenarios about political behaviour.

Public choice has not been widely applied to the study of the policy process. It assumes (along with much of the mainstream literature) that policy demands are self-interested, but also that the policy-makers – not only the political leaders, but also the bureaucrats – are driven by self-interest. Niskanen (1973) argued that bureaucrats are driven by self-interest to try to maximize the size and budgets of their agencies, which is an analysis which many find attractive, though it was not grounded in empirical research, and when some central agencies in the UK were reduced in size under the Thatcher government, attempts were made to explain this as the result of self-interested behaviour by bureaucrats seeking to maximize power rather than budgets (see Lewin 1991). Perhaps the most direct application has been the application of principal–agent theory in government, and the interest in contract-type relationships (including performance indicators) to achieve policy goals, e.g. contracts between a welfare department and a non-government body, or a government department and a university, or a minister and the departmental head. These reflect the public choice assumption that these relationships are between a principal with a goal to be achieved, and an agent, and that agents are self-interested and will 'shirk' unless there are explicit and inescapable controls.

The assumption that policy actors are driven by the desire to achieve some future benefit is axiomatic in a public choice framework, but is contested by writers like March and Olsen (1989, 2006), who contrast a 'logic of consequence' ('What do I want to achieve, and what is the best way to achieve it?') with a 'logic of appropriateness' ('What sort of situation is this?, What sort of person am I?, What does a person like me do in a situation like this?'). The implication is that since policy participants are engaged in continuing structured relationships – with political leaders, with other agencies, with organized interests, with constituents – they will seek to act in a way that is 'appropriate' for a person in this web of relationships, which brings us back to the question of what constitutes rational action in a policy context.

The policy agenda

The idea of a policy agenda, i.e. that there is a limited range of matters which can get policy attention, has had a strong appeal for people writing about policy (see Cobb and Elder 1972; Baumgartner and Jones 1991; Rochefort and Cobb 1994; Parsons 1995; Majone 2006). Much of the early interest was in the idea of agenda as a means of control; Schattschneider (1960: 71) argued that 'organization is the mobilization of bias. Some issues are organized into politics while others are organized out.' Crenson's (1971) study of policy on air pollution in two American cities argued that dominant industrial interests were able to exclude policy issues from consideration. Other writers took this further and explored the relationship between ideas and the institutional context in which they are considered, and Kingdon (1984) identified three distinct streams of action – the problem stream, the policy stream and the political stream – with the key question about agenda construction being how connections are made between these streams (see also Solesbury 1976). Here, the dominance of institutionalized expertise (like professions) is important (see Friedson 1986): which experts can define the nature of the problem? This aspect of agenda-setting has been explored by researchers developing an 'interpretive' approach to policy analysis (see Fischer and Forester 1993; Fischer 2003; Hajer and Wagenaar 2003), who have shifted the focus from 'agenda-setting' as a means of control to 'agenda construction' as a continuing, contested and ambiguous process.

Policy as collective action

There are many references in the policy literature to 'the policy-makers', the implication being that there are authority figures who make policy, perhaps assisted by expert advisers; Wildavsky (1979) saw policy analysis as 'speaking truth to power'. Radin (2000), however, found that policy analysts were not so much speaking truth to power as haggling with policy analysts in other agencies, and other researchers had noticed that policy workers were involved in continuing relationship with their counterparts in other organizations, i.e. that they were part of a stable pattern of collective action. Richardson and Jordan (1979) labelled this the 'policy community': the participants in each policy field who shared a concern with the subject (though not for the same reasons or with the same perspective) and were recognized as having a right to be involved. This term sparked immediate recognition, and there has been a great deal of writing on policy communities and its variants such as 'policy networks', 'issue networks' and 'sub-governments' (see Atkinson and Coleman 1992; Van Waarden 1992; Bogason 2006; Miller and Demir 2006). Sabatier and Jenkins-Smith (1993) identified 'advocacy coalition frameworks' within policy communities, and this term has also been widely used (see also Weible and Sabatier 2006). Thus policy researchers found themselves giving increasing attention to relationships among the policy participants, and to the idea of stable networks through which these participants operated (see Bogason 2006; Rhodes 2006; Raab and Kenis 2007).

Governance

The recognition of the interactive and negotiated dimension of policy work was reflected in the adoption of another new term:

'governance'. This had first been used in international relations to label 'governing without government', as it was put (Rosenau and Czempiel 1992): i.e. achieving rule without invoking the authority of the state. This metaphor was then applied to government at the national level (e.g. Peters and Pierre 1998). Rhodes (1997) argued that this characterized government in the UK, which had moved (or was moving) from 'government', achieved by authoritative direction, to 'governance', which was accomplished by the operation of self-organizing networks (though he appears now to have moved away from this contention: see Bevir *et al.* 2003). The term was adopted widely, both in the practice and in the analysis of governing, but with a bewildering variety of meanings. Some writers use the term to identify a particular way of governing, and some use it simply as a synonym for governing. The World Bank attempted to appropriate the term's vaguely positive overtones by describing its prescriptions for its client countries as 'good governance' (see Doornbos 2001). Van Keesbergen and Van Waarden (2004) give a good overview of the way the term is used, Pierre (2000) brings together some of the mainstream discussion, and Stoker (1998) identifies a core meaning which is useful for the analysis of policy, focusing on institutional complexity (see Kooiman 2003) and coordination without hierarchy. Attention is being given to 'multi-level government' (see Bache and Flinders 2004), networks (Börzel 1997, 1998) and to the international dimension of governing (see Larner and Walters 2006). There has been a particular focus on the development of new modes of governing in the European Union, with the 'open method of coordination' identified as a distinctively 'governance' way of governing (see Jordan *et al.* 2003; Borras and Jacobsson 2004).

Interpretive approaches

The concern with 'governance' has focused attention on the range of participants involved in the policy process. It has been paralleled by an interest in what it is that all these diverse stakeholders, with distinct and divergent understandings of the problem and agendas for action, are dealing with, i.e. what is the object of policy attention?

As we have already noted, 'environmental policy' did not emerge when governments recognized problems in a recognized sphere called 'the environment', but instead when activists drew attention to various things that were happening and sought to have them recognized as manifestations of a common problem: the stewardship of 'the environment'. The significance of this has been recognized and developed in an approach which has been called 'interpretive', 'argumentative' or 'narrative', and which examines how meaning is constituted – that is, how phenomena are labelled and set in context – in policy settings where meaning is often contested and ambiguous. There are many threads to this approach. It can be traced back to Edelman's work on symbol in politics (1964, 1971, 1977, 1988), and has also drawn on fine-grained research on the communication of meaning in practice – e.g. Forester (1981, 1983, 1993) and Healey (1992, 1993) – with Majone (1989) concluding that policy analysis has to be understood as a form of argumentation (see also Stone 1988, 1997). Fischer and Forester (1993) called this 'the argumentative turn in policy analysis', and their collection has a number of good case studies. The fundamentals were well expressed by Schön and Rein (1994), who pointed to the importance of 'naming and framing' the object of policy attention, and Roe (1994) identified 'storylines' in policy development, narratives which answered the question 'what's this all about?' On this perspective, many writers analysed policy development in terms of 'discourse' (e.g. Hajer 1995; Fischer and Hajer 1999), and Yanow (1996) pointed to the non-verbal ways in which meaning could be communicated in the policy process.

A number of fruitful lines of inquiry have emerged from this interpretive approach to policy. One has been the interest in 'policy learning', which recognized that policy development takes place in a world of interaction and discussion between policy workers, and can be seen as a process of learning (May 1992; Bennett and Howlett 1992; Stone 1999). This framework has been used in a succession of informative case studies (e.g. Hall 1993; Pal 1995; Mytelka and Smith 2002; Sanderson 2002; Lodge 2003; Meijerink 2005). It helps to throw light on the closely related question of the relationship between meaning and structure. Some see structure as reflecting meaning: Sabatier and Jenkins-Smith (1993) argue that policy development should be seen as a contest between 'advocacy coalitions' (see also Schlager 1995). At a very fundamental level, of course, organizations embody particular frameworks of meaning. For instance, health care is delivered through organizational frameworks dominated (in various ways) by particular occupational groups, of which doctors are the most evident, and the nature of care reflects the organization and its dominant framework of meaning. When HIV-AIDS became a policy question, gay groups in Australia contested the organizational and interpretive dominance of doctors, and to some extent were able to change the policy by establishing new organizational forms and interpretive frameworks (see Ballard 1989; for an example in a different setting, see Throgmorton 1991). The problematic relationship between interpretation and structure can also be seen in the feminist literature on policy work. The initial concern of feminist writers was with the way that feminist concerns were 'organized out' of policy concern, particularly through the definition of these issues as 'private' (see Pateman 1983; Pahl 1985). Subsequently, the focus shifted to what happened when these issues were 'organized in' – through policy changes, lawmaking and the organizational recognition of women's concerns. This did not always please the activists. Outshoorn (1991), for instance, described the status of women's issues in official arenas as 'issue perversion' and asked 'Is this what we wanted?' Jung (2002) gives an insightful comparison of the way feminists handled the transformation to 'insider' status in the contrasting political and social settings of Australia and Korea. For a practitioner account, see Eisenstein (1991).

Policy work

While Lasswell's original vision of a 'policy science' saw it as a means for the democratic interrogation of, and participation in, the work of government (see Auer 2006), it gave rise to a body of knowledge called 'policy analysis' which became (particularly in the United States) the basis for specialized employment – the 'policy analysis profession', as Radin (2000) calls it. Graduate schools offered courses in this subject, teaching students how to apply the methodology of the social sciences to make systematic comparisons of alternative courses of action so as to be able to advise the decision-makers of the optimal choice (see Weimer and Vining (2004) for a typical course text). People employed as policy analysts tended to find, first, that it was not clear that formal analysis was used to make decisions (see Weiss 1982, 1991), and second, that they were engaged in a range of activities (not just analysis) and often felt uncomfortable about the divergence between the systematic comparison that they had been trained to do and the activities in which they found themselves engaged (see Radin (2000) on the United States, Hoppe and Jeliazkova (2006) on the Netherlands). Noordegraaf (2000a, b) found that the work of policy manager revolved not around analysis but around negotiation: a world of meetings and documents. Other empirical studies draw attention to the emergence of new roles in policy work (e.g. Anderson 2006), to the management of discursive practices (Gill and Colebatch 2006; Tenbensel 2006), to the significance of organizational location (Hajer 2003b; Geuijen *et al.* 2006; Holland 2006), and to the way in which policy workers constituted the object of their attention (Colebatch 2002). It has become clear that the practices of the growing number of policy professionals cannot be inferred from the textbooks written to guide them.

But the professionalization of policy work in a technique labelled 'policy analysis' has not gone unchallenged, and there is a stream of writing asserting the need to see policy analysis as a democratic project. As we saw, the concern with 'policy agendas' reflected a concern for the way in which issues are recognized (or not). Lukes (1974) had argued that there were three levels of power: a surface level where overt conflicts were seen, a lower level where the powerful sought to avoid overt conflicts, and a deeper level at which power structures were reinforced through the manipulation of myths and symbols. This approach was developed by Benson, who argued that we need to think about a policy sector at three levels: a surface level of agencies with a concern for the issue, an interest structure of other groups which support and constrain them, and the 'rules of structure formation' which govern the way that the issue is understood and policy action is organized (Benson 1975, 1977, 1982).

In this context, many writers argue for a mode of policy analysis which incorporates all stakeholders through a process of 'discursive democracy' (Dryzek 1990; Throgmorton 1991; Fischer 1993; Fung and Wright 2003). It is argued that since not all the voices of the various stakeholders in a policy issue are likely to be heard, or heard equally (Hajer 2003a), policy analysis should be directed to generating outcomes through inclusive discourse (see Durning 1993; Kelly and Maynard-Moody 1993; for a contrary view, see Lynn 1999, also (reluctantly) Clemons and McBeth 2001).

Complementary approaches

In reviewing the literature on policy, it is also useful to take note of three areas of the social sciences which are not specifically addressed to policy but which are helpful in the analysis of the policy process: structuration, institutional organization theory, and governmentality. This is, of course, a personal selection: others might choose other themes which are equally worthy of attention.

Structuration

The sociologist Anthony Giddens addressed the question of the relationship between agency (what people do) and structure (the framework within which they do it), and argued that the two had to be seen as part of one process: the structure indicates what people (e.g. members of a family) should do; when they follow the indicated pattern (e.g. respond to family obligations), they 'reconstitute' the structure ('the family'). Giddens called this process 'structuration'. Applying this to policy, we can see that it is not the existence of some document which creates 'policy', but the impact this has on the behaviour of relevant people. Conversely, if we can see consistent patterns of behaviour ('this is how to handle this sort of problem'), we can talk about policy even in the absence of a formal document. We can see, though, that documents without behaviour, and behaviour without documents, could become problematic (see Giddens 1984; Parker 2000).

Institutional organization theory

Much writing on policy assumes organization, even when it is dealing with the absence of some sort of organizational behaviour, i.e. 'the problem of implementation'. In particular, it has difficulty dealing with relationships between organizations (because its focus is on the organization and its goals), and with the fact of time (i.e. that at any point, the participants are aware of both the past and the future, and this affects what they do in the present). Institutional organization theory (see DiMaggio and Powell 1991; Powell and DiMaggio 1991; Scott and Meyer 1991; Scott 2001) is helpful here because it recognizes that organizations are not just 'there', but are built up (institutionalized) over time. The process of institutionalization has three dimensions: one about the building-up of a shared interpretive schema ('cognitive'), one about the values which underlie this ('normative'), and one about the organizational forms through which these are given effect ('regulative'). This process can be seen at work across organizations ('organizational fields') as well as within them, and some of the most interesting applications to this to policy have to do with the way in which a range of organizations come to work together on policy questions in which they are all interested, but for different reasons. The institutional approach to organization helps us to understand why, for instance, non-governmental bodies which become part of government programmes start to resemble the government bodies they work with – a process labelled 'institutional isomorphism' by academics (see DiMaggio and Powell 1991; Keen 2002), and 'co-optation' by activists.

Governmentality

The governmentality approach draws on some of the work of Michel Foucault (1986; see also Burchell *et al.* 1991). Rose and Miller's article 'Political power beyond the state' (1992) is a good introduction to this approach, and Dean (1999) and Rose (1999) deal with it more extensively, and there is a comprehensive website on Foucault at http://www.michel-foucault.com.

Where do we place this book?

The last thing that the reader needs at this point are suggestions for further reading, but he or she would be justified in asking which of these approaches are used in this book. Of course, all of them have been taken note of in developing the approach to policy taken in this book, which might be called a 'social action' or 'social construction' analysis: it starts from the point that neither 'policy' nor the 'problems' to which it is addressed are natural phenomena with an existence of their own, independent of the participants; rather, they are produced by activities of the participants. For instance, 'the environment' is not a policy problem because of the smoke in the air; it is a problem because people notice the smoke in the air and want something done about it. So we have to ask not simply 'what is being done to address the problem?', but 'how is this problem perceived, and by whom, and in what way do they try to get support for action by drawing attention to "the problem of the environment"?' This approach draws on a body of theory about the nature of knowledge – including the work of writers like Kuhn (1962), Habermas (1984, 1989) and Foucault (1986) – and its application by writers like Berger and Luckman, who talk about 'the social construction of reality' (1975), Gusfield (1981) and Schön and Rein (1994). This approach is rather different from the mainstream of the policy literature, which focuses on how policy actors address problems, and is less concerned with how things become 'policy problems'.

7

What Does It Look Like on the Ground?

This book has taken a 'generic' approach to policy: it has talked about policy as such, and there has not been much reporting of 'actually existing policy', that is, live cases. This has been deliberate: this series is about concepts in the social sciences, and the book is concerned with policy as a concept – policy as a way of inter-rogating the world, and policy as a basis for action. This chapter relates this generic analysis of the concept to the empirical experi-ence of policy by discussing some examples of policy in specific contexts, focusing on health policy and policy in relation to climate change. It will show how using the three accounts of authoritative choice, structured interaction and social construction can help to make sense of the policy process. The empirical cases are from Australia, because that is where I live. Readers can then use this approach to investigate and analyse policy activity in their own countries.

Health policy

'Health policy' is an established policy field, an example of what we have called 'adjectival policy'. There are well-recognized partici-pants – ministers and secretaries of state and directors-general – university courses and texts, and a large literature with official statements of policy and a great deal of informed contribution and critique. There is a minister for health in the Australian Federal Government and in each of the eight state and territory govern-ments, and elections and parliamentary debates are marked by vigorous argument about 'health policy'. But Peter Baume – sur-geon turned politician turned academic, and a former minister for health in the Australian Federal Government – sounded a cautionary note, looking back on his own experience as a 'policymaker' in health:

> There has been no health policy from either major political party for
> many years. ... [We] do not collect routinely the information that
> would be needed for the measurement of many important health
> outcomes. ... [We] have forgotten about the achievement of health
> and have become obsessed with the treatment of illness, with salvage
> medicine, and with responding to the inevitable consequences of
> nutritional, alcoholic, driving and sexual excesses.
>
> (Baume 1995: 97–100)

Baume was writing in a reformist spirit, and much has changed since he wrote (particularly in relation to the collection of data), but he was making the important point that, while the policy subject is 'health', most of the activity which takes place under this heading is really about the maintenance of what might be called the 'sickness response industry'. The value attached to 'health' supports a discourse of 'health care' and an organizational framework (hospitals and doctors) for the delivery of this care. And governments have been strongly committed to supporting this system, with public expenditure on 'health' rising from 4 per cent of GDP in 1950 to 9 per cent in 2005/06 (Richardson 1984: 81; AIHW 2007: 78), but it is not clear that there has been a comparable increase in 'health', or how much such improvement as there has been in health has been the result of the increased expenditure on 'health care' (as opposed to changes in diet, smoking and lifestyle, for instance).

This presents a puzzle: there is a clear policy concern, and strong evidence of commitment, but it is not clear that the policy outcome has been commensurate with this commitment. This is why we need a more fine-grained analysis. We might start with the *social construction* of health policy: what is the nature of the problem that is being addressed?, what might be done about it?, and who should be doing it? At the micro or individual level, there is a sense of 'health' in terms of how well our bodies are coping with the demands of life, and 'ill-health' or 'sickness' as an upsetting of this ability to cope; the policy concern is that there should be some appropriate response to sickness. This is linked to another level (perhaps the 'meso' level), at which we find the many and varied forms of 'sickness response', bodies of knowledge and practice which define both the nature of the problem and the appropriate response – that is, 'health care': medicine, surgery, psychiatry, physiotherapy, nursing, etc. – which are increasingly being challenged and supplemented by the knowledge of 'user groups', organized around particular 'health conditions' (such as breast cancer) and mobilizing the knowledge of sufferers, carers and survivors. There is also an increasingly significant body of knowledge about personal practice rather than professional intervention, and focused on diet, exercise and the management of the self. At the macro level, there are several overlapping understandings, one about the health of the whole population and the reasons for variation in health. This is conducted among experts and draws on survey data, statistics and epidemiology (the branch of medicine concerned with the incidence of disease), and is likely to be concerned with the relative effectiveness, and the cost, of different sorts of treatment, and also of the non-medical factors that affect health status, such as diet and smoking. This expert discourse, which is focused on the prevention of illness rather than its cure, is likely to be only imperfectly related to another discourse about the provision of health care which is of immediate concern to political leaders: how health care is distributed, funded and managed. And here, political leaders will be sensitive to their constituents: what does the public see as important matters of policy concern in relation to health?

We can see that there is a range of understandings about health and policy, and that each is linked to a pattern of *structured interaction*. At the micro, or personal, level, members of the public want to be confident that the appropriate care will be available if they need it, and having a local doctor's clinic and a convenient hospital will be reassuring to them. But medical care is specialized and delivered through complex institutional forms including hospitals, medical faculties, research institutes, professional associations and advocacy groups as well as government health agencies, and the policy process is concerned with the place of each of these and the claims that they make on public attention and resources. And at the macro level, the existence of different discourses about needs, demands and effectiveness would make enacting policy as *authoritative choice* contentious, contested, ambiguous and provisional.

So, making policy in relation to health is not so much the solution of a known problem as the development of a 'work in progress'. In nineteenth-century Australia, it would have been difficult to talk of health policy because in the dominant social construction neither health nor health care was seen as having much to do with government (apart from the government's responsibility for the health of convicts); rather, it was seen as a matter for the individual or the community. Health care was provided by doctors or pharmacists, who charged fees, although community organizations called 'friendly societies' were formed to provide an alternative form of care, collecting weekly subscription from members, who were then entitled to free treatment at a regular clinic. Hospitals were formed mostly by community organizations or religious bodies; they received some government support, but were not run by government (and in any case, tended to be seen as institutions for the poor: middle- and upper-class people expected to be treated at home). Health became a matter of policy concern in the late nineteenth century, when a Board of Health was established by the New South Wales government as a result of an outbreak of epidemic disease. The Board, however, was concerned not with 'sickness response' but with the environmental determinants of health, and initiated a programme of drainage, rodent control and slum clearance.

Through the twentieth century, particularly in the latter half, health became established as a policy concern, and the diverse practices of care were increasingly integrated into an official framework. The social construction of health was still focused on the provision of treatment, but this came to be seen as a matter of government concern, and the constitution was amended by referendum in 1946 to allow the Federal Government to subsidize medical and pharmaceutical costs. Australians also accepted measures to control the spread of tuberculosis, which included compulsory X-rays of the entire adult population and compulsory hospitalization of those carrying the disease, and extensive programmes of immunization were carried out through the school system. The institutional structures of care were drawn more into the official realm. Hospitals became increasingly funded and controlled by government, and their local governing bodies were marginalized or abolished. The Federal Government became increasingly involved in funding and control, and by 2005/06 was contributing 43 per cent of the cost of health care, with state/local governments paying 25 per cent and non-governmental sources (e.g. insurance companies and individuals) 32 per cent (AIHW 2007: 20). Insurance for health care was subsidized by government in various ways, and a national insurance scheme was also established.

There was more surveillance: data-gathering on the health status of the population, scrutiny of hospital standards, and even of the practices of doctors. By the close of the century, observers could talk about 'the Australian health system', and there was quite a lot of data on health, health needs and health services (partly in response to the concerns articulated by people like Peter Baume). The data-gathering also reflected the influence of an international agenda among health professionals (and the World Health Organization) of 'health for all', and a range of programmes emerged to focus attention on improving health rather than treating sickness. But while there has been a good deal of rhetorical support for this broader agenda, government spending is dominated by the maintenance of the sickness response industry: the hospitals and the doctors. The social construction of health is still focused on treatment, and political leaders wanted to be associated with the provision of medical care: more hospitals, more nurses, more technology. There is broad acceptance of the health benefits of quitting smoking, limiting alcohol consumption and improving diet, but not at the expense of the provision of hospital care. Public opinion polls show health and Medicare (the government scheme which subsidizes medical treatment) is rated as the second-most important political issue, and three-quarters of those interviewed said that it influenced their voting choice (Gray 2001). Waiting lists for elective surgery, for instance, are particularly sensitive politically, and because this is how the voters see the issue, there is not much interest among legislators, or most ministers, in restricting service provision. This is why (as Baume admitted) political leaders were focused not so much on achieving health as on providing treatment and working out how to pay for it. The medical profession has proved very skilful at manipulating the media and fanning public anxiety, and while political leaders could from time to time be persuaded to endorse efforts to promote health (e.g. by reducing smoking), such campaigns would be swept from the front page by suggestions that Hospital X would have to reduce its services because it had overspent its budget.

This does not mean that political leaders have not been engaged in activities of *authoritative choice*: making decisions and declaring objectives. Baume relates that, in 1988, the health ministers of the Federal and state/territory governments endorsed a set of goals for the health system:

The goals themselves were modest and most related to relatively low-cost and low-technology issues – the prevention of avoidable violent death, the avoidance of the worst disorders of nutrition, the immunisation of more of our children against preventable infectious disease, the prevention of dental caries, the treatment and detection of mild hypertension, and many more relatively simple measures.

An amount of money ($39 million over three years) was made available, but activities under that program were not internalised into hospital and medical management systems. Almost all of the modest goals set in 1988 remain unmet (with the exception of childhood immunisation) and will remain unresolved until the systems themselves are told that the achievement of better health is one outcome on which they will be judged.

(Baume 1995: 100)

But the refocusing of the policy discourse continued, and in 1994 the ministers endorsed a National Health Policy, saying:

The development of a National Health Policy is an acknowledgement by governments of the need to re-orient policies and programs towards improving health rather than simply providing health care services.

(Commonwealth of Australia 1994: 16)

Working groups of representatives of governments, medical organizations and consumer groups drafted detailed statements of goals, targets and indicators of progress, articulating a focus on improved health outcomes. What is less clear is whether this new commitment meant shifting resources from existing services. Policy is concerned with the structured interaction between stakeholders, and existing programmes will usually have their supporters. Enunciating a concern with health outcomes is one thing; closing a hospital in order to achieve them is quite another.

As the twenty-first century began, Australia was spending roughly the OECD average on health care and enjoying slightly better than average health, although Aboriginal Australians had much worse health, often at Third World levels (AIHW 2007, 2008). It was not clear, though, how much the outcomes were related to spending on health care, as opposed to changes in the contextual determinants of health, such as diet, smoking, exercise, alcohol consumption, employment and social class. Government documents recognized, for instance, that much of the improvement in male life expectancy was probably due to men giving up smoking (AIHW 2008). But the structured commitments are to the provision of care: in 2005/06, the greatest item of health expenditure in Australia was Hospitals, with Medical Services not far behind; together, these two accounted for about 70 per cent of health expenditure, with another 15 per cent for medication; Community and Public Health (which includes efforts to reduce smoking) accounted for about 7 per cent. It may be that a programme of early detection and careful self-management is more cost-effective than surgery as a method of reducing deaths from coronary heart disease, but the coronary surgery units are there in the hospitals and treating patients, and it is difficult to shut such a unit down in order to fund a programme that in ten years' time will have eliminated much of the demand for such a unit. So there is constant argument about the relative worth of different approaches to health, and technologies of measurement such as the 'disability-adjusted life year' have been devised as a basis for the comparison of the worth of, for instance, a heart transplant programme with a programme of education and domiciliary care for people with coronary heart disease.

This means that policy activity is taking place in different forms at different locations. In the social construction of the policy problem, there has been a broad shift of perspective among the policy practitioners, and to some extent among health practitioners themselves, with a greater concern for outcomes, an insistence on evidence that therapeutic activities will produce better outcomes, and an awareness of the possibility of improving health by changing lifestyle. At the same time, for most members of the public, the role of the government is still seen as ensuring the provision of hospitals and medical care, and this is reflected both in the structured commitments to the organizations through which care is provided and in the public statements of political leaders.

So, policy participants – in Federal and state health departments, professional organizations, research institutes and non-governmental organizations – therefore look for ways to make links between social construction, structured interaction and authoritative choice, and to change the nature of the discourse to enable a restructuring of commitments and a change in the allocation of resources (Degeling 2001). There are a number of avenues through which they do this. One is by exercising *tighter control over the provision of care*, strengthening the authority of management, particularly in controlling costs. This has meant involving health professionals in the management of resources, which challenges the idea of the separation of policy and implementation.

> [W]hen a physician joins a policy committee (determining criteria for a home oxygen program for advanced lung disease, say, or sitting on a hospital committee that will restrict the pharmacopoeia in various ways), he or she is serving as a technical expert in the development of health policy. ...
>
> Some doctors feel that the role of the technical expert should not be required of them: 'Leave that to the administrators! If our budget for dialysis is to be cut next year, let someone else cut it! It's nothing to do with me!'
>
> (Leeder 1999: 86)

One strategy for compelling the clinicians to take responsibility for the resource consequences of their decisions has been 'casemix funding', where the hospital receives a lump sum (based on average costs) for the case, rather than payment based on the amount of treatment. There have also been moves to strengthen the surveillance of the quality of care, in the wake of scandals which showed that traditional professional self-discipline has tended to protect the professionals more than the patients.

At the same time, there are continuing efforts to *change the nature of the discourse*, so that the focus of attention is expanded to take in the contextual determinants of health (such as diet and smoking) as well as the measures taken in response to ill-health. In 2008, the newly elected Prime Minister made a speech condemning 'binge drinking' among young people, and launched a number of policy initiatives which reinforced the importance of alcohol abuse in the health policy agenda. There have also been a number of public inquiries convened on a range of topics, not simply to generate advice for government but also to change public understandings and provide a location for interaction among stakeholders (see Degeling *et al.* 1993). There have been moves, too, to create new visibilities and measurements with which the appropriateness of clinical judgements can be challenged, such as the 'disability-adjusted life years' previously mentioned. Policy workers have sponsored studies of clinical variation, technologies of measurement for quality control, and 'evidence-based medicine' as a way of altering the terms of the debate. There have also been moves to widen the range of voices which are taken seriously in policy discourse, and organizations which promote alternatives to the dominant model of medical provision – e.g. by focusing on community health, quality control, peer review, health consumers and the professionalization of nursing – get official support and funding. The Health Consumers Forum, established in 1987, has been a focal point for user groups and a stimulus for the involvement of consumer views throughout the health care domain.

Another reform theme has been *structural change*, particularly in creating linkages among specialized services, between these services and related services such as welfare and housing, and between them and the population that they serve. The state of Victoria amalgamated its health and social welfare departments to create a single (and massive) Department of Human Services. On a smaller scale, the organizational base for health services has been changed from service point (e.g. the hospital) to area in an attempt to focus on the health status of the whole population (i.e. the outcome) rather than the efficiency of the particular organization (the process). But perhaps the most significant reform move (in terms of traditional thinking about policy) has been the incorporation of non-official forms of organizing in the recognized health care system. These may be organizations based on locality, religion, or (increasingly) a particular disease or disability. These have been particularly evident in areas where the sufferers may have tended to avoid conventional medical care, such as mental health, drug abuse and HIV-AIDS, but, increasingly, these groups grow up around particular conditions, are recognized by the therapists, and incorporated into official decision-making (where they lobby for 'their' clinicians in the competition for resources). They have peak bodies to represent them to government, and often receive government grants. The Breast Cancer Action Group NSW, for instance, was formed in the state of New South Wales when one woman wrote a newspaper article about her experience of breast cancer, and received such a response that she convened a public meeting. This was attended by 125 people, who decided to form an organization, the Breast Cancer Action Group NSW. They identified the stakeholders relevant to breast cancer, and asked for representation on relevant bodies. Within three years, they were represented on 45 committees through the health system, putting the viewpoint of patients, and had produced (in conjunction with the Health Care Complaints Commission) a leaflet of advice for women diagnosed with breast cancer. They received grants for particular projects, but they subcontracted these to outside workers. They did not seek funding for the group as such, nor did they employ paid staff, because they did not want to become dependent on government or industry funding. They preferred to remain a network of activists, sharing their common experience, and bringing it to bear at relevant points in the health system. This group realized that many of its members' issues were cancer generic, that is, shared by all cancer sufferers. They linked with similar groups to form Cancer Voices, a state-level peak body representing more than 80 organizations. Cancer Voices provides trained consumer representatives to sit on 112 committees and research groups. There is no tally of the number of non-governmental organizations involved in the health system in this way, but in the mental health area alone, over 500 non-governmental bodies are officially recognized.

Here, we can see the link between social construction and structured interaction. Refocusing of policy on improving health outcomes involves the identification of the sources of health risk, and leads to the adoption of goals which go well beyond the delivery of services, such as:

- 'reduce the prevalence of smoking';
- 'increase participation in regular physical activity';
- 'reduce the prevalence of obesity among adults'.

Here, we are being drawn back to the 'governmentality' perspective, which starts with Foucault's description of government as 'the conduct of conduct', and looks at the way in which 'state action' comes to focus on the shaping of conduct. The policy workers know that much of the source of ill-health lies in the way that people live their lives, and they look for ways to bring about changes. For instance, they note that smoking has declined most among males, and identify younger women and Aboriginals as the 'priority population', i.e. the people who are resisting the newly articulated model of 'healthy living'. This calls for an understanding of why these people, for instance, continue to smoke, and policy workers try to identify the forces that might lead to changes in values and behaviour, and look for structures which might influence people's behaviour. For instance, in order to reduce sporting injuries, the Better Health strategy proposes:

> Form a national coalition of key stakeholders from the injury pre-
> vention, sports and recreation bodies, and government agencies to

devise a National Sports Safety Strategy, and to coordinate its implementation.

(Commonwealth of Australia 1994: 212)

This is to be supported by financial incentives:

Introduce an accreditation scheme for sport and recreation bodies which ties accreditation to funding, and includes benchmarks for injury prevention.

(Commonwealth of Australia 1994: 213)

Here, the policy task is concerned less with what the government does itself, and more with the impact it has on what other 'governing bodies' do; the governmentality school calls this 'governing at a distance' (see Rose and Miller 1992).

So, seeing health policy as 'what the government wants or decides' is not very helpful either in explaining the action or in indicating to the practitioner what action would be effective. There are existing structures of practice in place which are themselves claims for commitment of resources, and which are also being challenged by countervailing discourses from the users of these structures. But at the same time, we can see that this goal model of policy is being mobilized to challenge practice and the institutionalized domination of the doctors – the established pattern of structured interaction. The public commitment of the ministers to a set of outcome-based goals, with specific targets and indicators attached to them, is evidence of the way that the changing social construction of health policy is having an effect on 'the structured commitment of important resources', requiring participants making claims for resources to justify those claims in terms of health outcomes. The promotion of 'evidence-based medicine', for instance, challenges doctors to show that the therapies they are accustomed to using do in fact make a difference.

Concerns about health are institutionalized in different ways, and governments come to be associated with them; statements about why governments are (or are not) involved ('policy') can be significant, but they have to be understood as part of a process in which the claims of different sorts of activity for official support contend with one another, and shared understandings emerge about what is seen as 'health care', how it should be organized, and what role government should have in it. We can see that authoritative choice, structured interaction and social construction are all significant (but incomplete) accounts in the analysis of health policy.

There are processes of choice, of negotiation and of 'collective puzzling' (Heclo 1974) as the participants mobilize the concepts of 'health' and 'policy' in support of their various projects. The important thing for the analyst of health policy is to recognize this interplay.

Climate change policy

> *Everyone talks about the weather, but no one does anything about it.*
>
> *– Mark Twain*

The climate is not a traditional area for policy-making. With rare exceptions, policy-makers have assumed that the climate is one of the givens of life. Scientists could, to some extent, explain why we get particular weather patterns, but while this knowledge might help policy-makers by, for instance, predicting floods, for the most part it did not relate to policy agendas. Now, though, climate change has emerged as a policy issue. It is now widely accepted that the way in which we use energy in its different forms has an effect on global temperatures which is already changing the climate, and could result in the melting of the polar ice caps, a rise in sea levels, and a range of other undesirable outcomes, and that governments therefore need to act to prevent this happening.

Here again, we can see the connection between social construction, structured interaction and authoritative choice in the development of policy. Traditionally, most people did not see the climate as something that the government could do anything about, and political leaders did not see any need to have policies in relation to climate, other than measures to protect people from the consequences, such as limiting house-building on flood-prone land, or building dams in order to 'drought-proof' the cities. There was little awareness that the practices of government might themselves be promoting climate change (e.g. requiring farmers to cut down all the trees in order to get title to their land) or exacerbating its effects (e.g. allowing upstream farmers to extract water from the rivers, or to prevent water reaching the rivers).

What changed this was the increasing awareness among specialists – scientists and environmental activists – of climate change and how it was related to the practices of government and of everyday life, and how this changed awareness came to be significant to the 'policy-makers'. Through the 1970s, there was increasing discussion among scientists about what different forms of measurement showed about the earth's climate and how these should be interpreted, and this was noticed by environmental activists who were already concerned about the human impact on the earth's capacity to cope. At the same time, the issue of climate change was becoming more noticed in the 'ordinary knowledge' of non-specialists, particularly as what had traditionally been seen as 'natural disasters' – e.g. floods, fires and typhoons – seemed to become more frequent. This stimulated interest in the explanation of climate change and whether this should become a matter of collective concern, and the generation of 'causal stories' (Stone 1989; Roe 1994) about what is happening, why, and who should be held responsible – the 'social construction' of the policy issue.

The question was how these 'causal stories' about climate change might have an impact on public consciousness and the attention span of political leaders. Here (unusually), the scientists already had some experience of organizing for policy, gained in the 1970s and 1980s when they had drawn attention to an emerging hole in the ozone layer above the earth, and governments took action at an international level to limit the use of the chlorofluorocarbons which were seen as the cause (see Haas 1992b). This showed scientists the potential impact of an 'epistemic community' of scientists who had a common understanding of the problem (Haas 1992a), and the importance of organizing at an international level. International scientific discussion played a major role in the development of climate change as a policy issue: scientists were appointed to the Intergovernmental Panel on Climate Change, whose 2007 report on the nature, sources and likely consequences of climate change provided the explanation and justification for the policy changes that political leaders came to accept. As Professor Ross Garnaut put it in presenting his report on climate change to the Australian Government: 'those of us who are not climate scientists have no choice but to accept the weight of scientific evidence' (Morton 2008).

But this scientific evidence implicated most areas of Australian life in the process of climate change: motorists who drive to work rather than taking public transport; town planners, developers and transport authorities whose combined activities have meant that public transport is not an option for many workers; electricity authorities who generate power by burning coal; factories whose chimneys emit pollutants; farmers who replace forests with wheat fields; households who use clothes dryers: the challenge to existing social practice was immense. Discussion of the problem came to focus on carbon dioxide, and the impact of any given practice on the environment could be stated in terms of tonnes of carbon dioxide emitted. Here was a measure which was easily understood, and used to evaluate the effectiveness of proposals.

But who would be responsible for policy development in relation to climate change, and what ability would they have to bring about the changes in practice which would make a difference to climate change? Policy development at this level would involve renegotiating the terms on which people conducted their work and their daily lives: it would be an immense, contested, continuing and ambiguous exercise, both within Australia and at the international level.

Here again, policy development begins with the social construction of the problem rather than with the identification of options for responding to it. As we saw, there had been a growing consensus among scientists that it was the impact of human activity that was producing climate change, and that this would have adverse effects for all humanity, and through the efforts of environmental activists, this was increasingly accepted in Australian public opinion. But would people accept a reduced standard of living – higher prices for petrol, electricity, food, public transport, etc. – in order to avert catastrophic climate change? How would political leaders interpret the situation? There was growing acceptance among political leaders that climate change was an issue on which they could and should act, but this was not universal – the conservative Federal Government elected in 1996 remained sceptical of the climate change argument, but the Labor opposition made it a central element in the policy platform on which it defeated the conservatives in the 2007 elections. But this electoral victory did not resolve the issue, which remained an area of dispute and ambiguous outcomes.

The issue was not simply 'what is happening to the climate?', but also 'who should do something about it?', which led to 'what is fair?' Here, international comparisons became important. After all, the United States, with 4 per cent of the world's population, produces 23 per cent of the emissions (OECD/IEA 1992); why shouldn't they reduce their emissions more than other, less polluting countries? Why should Australian farmers be prevented from clearing the trees from their farms because British and German farmers cleared their trees hundreds of years ago? Developing countries fear that the environment is an issue which the developed world uses in an attempt to prevent them industrializing in the uncontrolled, polluting way that the West did. As an exporting country, Australia has been concerned that greenhouse controls may be imposed in Australia but not in the countries whose exports compete with ours, meaning that Australia will be at a cost disadvantage. And, of course, Australia is a major exporter of coal, which is one of the main sources of carbon dioxide emissions.

This brings us to the central dilemma of climate change as a policy problem: the effectiveness of what we do depends on what others do, but we cannot be sure about what they will do when we decide what we will do: this is the classic 'prisoner's dilemma', and this is why the Garnaut Report (Commonwealth of Australia 2008) to the Australian Government described climate change as a 'diabolical' policy problem. If Australia reduces its emissions but the United States, China and India do not, the impact on climate change of Australia's policy actions will be almost zero: why endure the pain if there will be no gain? Should countries take a lead in the hope that this will induce others to follow, or should they wait for others to move first? This is an ethical–practical question, and there has been wide disagreement about this in Australia, with the Federal Government and its principal adviser (Ross Garnaut) being prepared to move first, the Federal opposition being uncertain whether to move or to wait for others, and one conservative commentator arguing that since the likelihood that other countries will make equivalent cuts is small, any cuts to emissions by Australia should be equally small (Ergas 2008).

But while consultants can argue that the government should do nothing, in the real world, policy ideas are in circulation, and policy participants respond to them in different ways. There is, in any case, no single, detached participant called 'the government' making an overarching policy decision; many of the areas of practice are, under Australia's constitution, responsibilities of the state governments, and some – such as the design of domestic appliances or the energy efficiency of buildings or the fuel consumption of cars – are areas which, until recently, have attracted little attention from any level of government. The more that attempts to control emissions involved making changes to the practices of industries or households, the more important it became to develop new structures of authority which could have an impact on these practices, and these were likely to involve non-governmental participants in the creation and practice of policy. The initial moves for policy development involved negotiations between the Federal Government and the state and territory governments, since many of the activities under examination were the constitutional responsibility of the states. From these negotiations, a Comonwealth Greenhouse Office was established in 1998 in the Federal Department of the Environment, and a National Greenhouse Strategy was promulgated. The strategy contained a range of measures to limit greenhouse emissions, including:

* reforms to the energy and gas industries;
* more use of renewable energy sources;
* improvements in public transport;
* development of standards and codes of practice for increased energy efficiency in industry, housing and commercial buildings;
* controls on land clearing by farmers.

Achieving change, however, required negotiations with industry, formation of consultative bodies to gain acceptability for the measures proposed, and public education campaigns – all of which were contentious and vulnerable to derailing by affected interests. Some connections are easier to make than others. Since building standards were already controlled, amending the standards to promote energy efficiency was relatively easy. Where possible, policy workers seek out representatives of areas of practice such as industry associations or bodies defining professional standards, with whom they can negotiate codes of conduct. For instance:

> Work is being undertaken to improve the efficiency of fertiliser spreading and handling to reduce the amount entering waterways; this includes the development of a fertiliser spreading accreditation program and codes of conduct.
>
> (Commonwealth of Australia 1997: 62)

Trying to achieve changes in daily life was much more difficult; there was no professional body which could define the norm for taking a shower, and to persuade people to take shorter showers, a more efficient shower head was designed, which the water authorities offered free to customers. During long, dry summers, restrictions were imposed on the use of water for watering gardens and washing cars, but these were seen as temporary measures, to be eased when the reservoirs were replenished.

Much more intractable, though, were the entrenched interests of industry, particularly coal and electricity, where governments (usually state) either owned the industry or were closely involved with its success. In the state of New South Wales, where the government was attempting to privatize its coal-burning power stations, the state government was vehemently opposed to controls on carbon emissions, because the more rigorous these were, the less the government could expect to receive for the sale of the power stations.

At the same time, policy activity was going on at the international level, and the Australian Government had to respond to this. The activities of the scientists and activists had led to a series of international conferences which drafted and, in 1992, adopted a Framework Convention on Climate Change under the auspices of the United Nations, signed by 154 countries and the European Community. In this Convention, the industrialized countries agreed to adopt measures which would reduce their emissions of greenhouse gases to 1990 levels by 2000. No specific targets or binding commitments were included, but these were added in the Kyoto Protocol of 1997. The conservative Australian Government (following the US lead) refused to sign the Protocol, but at the Bali Climate Change Conference in 2007, Australia's new Labor government made a very public declaration of Australia's intention to sign the Kyoto Protocol. By 2008, the new government had announced its intention to introduce an 'emissions trading scheme', under which the government would set limits on the amount of carbon which would be emitted, and issue licences to existing emitters, which could be bought and sold. This would then create a market in these licences, which would mean that the level of carbon emission was being controlled, and that who was doing the emitting would be governed by market forces, not government licensing.

We can see here the interplay between authoritative choice and structured interaction: the authority of government is being mobilized, but as a way of changing the structured interaction between the participants. And it has also been mobilized to change the nature of the social construction of the issue. When the Federal Government appointed Professor Garnaut to report on climate change, it launched a process of public inquiry and discussion which, over a year or more, focused attention on the argument and what could or should be done. This was an exercise in the social construction of the issue: it did not resolve it, but it helped to frame the debate and to generate among the participants, inside and outside of government, a sense of the parameters of the possible. This is the 'collective puzzling' which Heclo (1974) noted: the process of public argumentation through which the parameters of what is problematic, what is possible and what is reasonable are argued out.

We should not see the actors in policy development as 'the government' or 'non-government'. There is not one government and one mind, but many governmental forms, at different levels, and many of the voices heard in them are not governmental. Creating policy to govern human activity in relation to climate change did not begin with governments, but with scientists and activists, and these people remained significant participants with a place in official forums; even the high-level UN Climate Change Conference in Bali in 2007 had a large number of non-governmental participants. Environmental agencies may be trying to impose controls on carbon emissions, electricity agencies may be trying to avoid them – and both agencies will be looking for non-governmental support.

The climate change case brings home to us how much policy is about framing, i.e. constructing an account which makes a particular sort of action appropriate. And the new account has to be superimposed on top of other competing meanings, and these other meanings do not disappear; they remain there, with their organizational structures and their underlying values, resisting the impact of the new policy measures. The question is how the different discourses of the participants are related to one another in the policy process: what ways of talking about the issue are acceptable and constructive, and what ways are seen as obstructive – what Fairclough calls 'the order of discourse' (see Chouliaraki and Fairclough 1999; Fairclough 2001).

Moreover, this framing of policy is not independent of the social practice through which it is produced. For instance, as part of the global warming policy, all state governments introduced measures to limit clearing tree cover from farms, but this was resisted by farming interests, and government agencies were reluctant to coerce their traditional constituents. But Halpin (2002) found that when the farmers' association agreed to nominate farmers to local committees to prepare local vegetation control plans, intending to withdraw them later on the basis that the plans were unworkable, these farmers became enthusiastic supporters of the plans which they had helped to prepare, and the association was unable to carry out its plan for a strategic boycott of the process.

We can see here that policy development takes place at different levels, often at the same time, and that each of our three accounts illuminates a distinct aspect of the process. Political leaders can make decisions (authoritative choice), but the sorts of decisions that they can make are constrained by the continuing interplay among the participants (structured interaction) and the shared under-standings about the nature of the problem and the appropriate response (social construction).

This means that the relationship between policy and government is a complex one. Policy development on climate change in Aus-tralia did not begin with government, nor did it end with a government decision, but began with concerned specialists and in many ways has been sustained and made inescapable at the inter-national (i.e. intergovernmental) level. But the idea of government has been important, and painfully negotiated compromises have to be 'enacted' with the authority of government, at both the national and international level. In a way, government is pivotal without being central: the action revolves around government, but progress depends on the extent to which bodies which are not subject to direction by government can be woven into a framework under which the policy concern is seen as being 'under control'. We have become accustomed to thinking of 'the state' as a body with the capacity to direct, but in the two cases we have examined here, state direction ('authoritative choice') is only a part, and not even the major part, of the process of making policy.

Further reading

This chapter shows how this approach to the analysis of policy can be applied in specific contexts. The question for the reader is now 'how does this account of Australian policy practice compare with policy in these fields (or with policy in other areas) in my own country?' The task is to find the evidence – through reading, experience, and the interrogation of everyday practice – which will help to answer this question.

8

How Do You Do It?

Policy as activity

Policy is a concept in the social sciences, but it is also something that people *do*. For some people, it is a specialized form of work: there are people with titles like Policy Analyst and Policy Manager, and organizational forms like the Policy Branch, and there are many other people, paid and unpaid, who are working at policy. But what are they doing?

It depends on whether we are thinking of policy as an outcome or as a process. There are things called 'policies' – the national competition policy, the state planning policy, the school discipline policy – and common sense suggests that policy activity means the making of these policies: policy as an *outcome*. This implies the existence of a formal statement of the policy, and focuses attention on the activities of the authoritative decision-makers (because they make the statement), and on the extent to which the stated policy has been carried out (implementation) and to which it has achieved its objectives (evaluation).

To the extent that participants are engaged in the production of these documents, they are seen as being engaged in policy activity. Framing the policy process as a succession of stages (see Chapter 4) labels their activities in terms of these stages:

- defining the problem;
- identifying alternative responses/solutions;
- evaluating options;
- deciding;
- implementing;
- evaluating outcomes.

This looks like a clear sequence of activities culminating in an authoritative document – an outcome (even if many practitioners might find it difficult to allocate the tasks of their working day into one or other of these categories). However, many people (including, probably, most practitioners) would say that it is not sufficient just to have a statement of policy. That statement has to have an impact on what people do, and to achieve this, we have to pay attention to the pattern of action of which the formal statement is a part. Policy, they argue, is a *process* which begins long before the formal statement, goes on long after it has been proclaimed and may not be accompanied by a formal statement at all. Even if there is a formal statement, it will not express the complexity of the action. There are many participants, and they all have varied agendas, so the policy task is to pull them together. Typically, it goes on over a long period of time, and involves a great deal of interaction among the participants. One reason for this is that the participants have different reasons for being involved and different ways of seeing the problem and evaluating possible courses of action. Consequently, policy work involves constructing an account of the problem and the response to be taken which is acceptable to a wide range of stakeholders. On this perspective, doing policy is not primarily about promulgating formal statements, but about negotiating with a range of significant participants so that when (or if) formal statements are made, they accurately reflect the concerns of the participants and what they have agreed to do, and are likely to have a significant impact on what they actually do.

Of course, the two perspectives are complementary, not contradictory: the busy discussion, negotiation and consensus-seeking are the means (process) through which the participants seek an end (outcome) which can be enacted as a 'decision' of the government. It is another illustration of the distinction between the authoritative choice and the structured interaction accounts of policy (see Chapter 3). In the authoritative choice account, the focus is on the outcome, and policy activity is seen in terms of 'decision support' (i.e. identifying and comparing options, checking that decisions have been executed and that they have had the desired effect). In the structured interaction account, the focus is on the range of participants, the diversity of their agendas and the limited capacity to impose a solution by the use of authorized decisions; and policy activity is seen more in terms of process: negotiation, coalition-building, the construction of meaning, and the generation and

ratification of agreed courses of action. This tension between outcome and process is understood by the practitioners, even if they do
not always give voice to it (remembering, as they do, that what they
say is itself part of the action). Political leaders generally recognize
that while they can issue commands to some people, they must also
deal in some way with people whom they cannot command. And
the negotiators operating on the horizontal plane (see Figure 3.1 in
Chapter 3) recognize that their activity must in some way be related
to the pattern of authorized decision, e.g. by being described as the
'preparation' of a policy.

So, rather than trying to track the making of policy by looking
for 'the policy-makers' – i.e. assuming that there are particular
systemic tasks to be done and looking around to find who is doing
them – we need to ask what the things are that people do which
produce policy: that is, to see policy as a pattern of activity.

Policy is the work of many hands, but all activity is not the same,
nor is it equally significant. For many of the participants, participation in policy is an occasional activity, sparked by a particular
event (such as the building of a freeway), or a by-product of some
other interest. For others, policy activity is a skilled occupation:
they are likely to be engaged in it full-time, and to be paid for it.
Sometimes, their policy work will be reflected in their job title (e.g.
'Manager, Policy'); sometimes the title will give no clue (e.g.
'Secretary'). Some hold no official position, but can play a very
significant role in particular circumstances. Here again, it is useful
to think in terms of the three accounts of the policy process –
authoritative choice, structured interaction and social construction
– and to ask: how do these illuminate what people do to 'make
policy'?

Authoritative choice

The authoritative choice account (like the other two accounts)
frames the action in a particular way, identifies the participants and
validates practices. Because it relates to very visible and public
forms of practice, it seems only common sense. It seems obvious
that ministers (or cabinets) make decisions, legislators pass statutes,
boards of directors approve proposals, national councils pass
resolutions, and that in this way they 'make policy'. This account
frames the policy process in a way which fits the public presentation
of government. It focuses on the idea of decision, and identifies the

people who can be appropriately involved and the practices that should be followed. The people are defined in terms of their standing in relation to legitimate authority, usually derived from the processes of representative government (though it may also come from hereditary rank). There are, for a start, the leaders themselves, who are seen as the 'decision-makers'. They may have been elected to the legislature, and in countries with a Westminster system, become ministers; in other systems, they may have been appointed to a leadership position by the people who won the election. In any case, they hold their position by virtue of demonstrated public support, and may lose it if that support fades.

In many cases (particularly in government) leaders are surrounded by aides – people recruited (often on a temporary basis) to serve the leader personally, and who can expect to lose their jobs if the leader changes, or loses confidence in them (see Walter 1986; Holland 2002; Maley 2003). They are likely to be political allies of the leader, and to see themselves as 'street-wise', drawing on their own intuition more than on expert knowledge (see Maley 2000), but some may be recruited on the basis of their expert knowledge, e.g. a new minister for housing seeking to recruit an aide with specialist knowledge of housing to be an alternative to the department as a source of expert advice. Or they may come from a lobby group and be recruited to strengthen order by maintaining good relations with organized interests. In any case, they tend to become involved in a succession of ad hoc activities: troubleshooting. Aides are likely to be particularly concerned with ensuring that the actions of other participants do not impact adversely on their own leader; one ex-aide argued that, with increasing media scrutiny, aides are focused on 'winning each day's headline' (Anderson 2006). This reflects the influence of the media, which is likely to be mobilizing the authoritative choice account to critique the performance of government in the light of the policy undertakings given at the last election. So, leaders and their staff are likely to be active in making public declarations of policy, and looking for opportunities to take new policy initiatives. They will insist on the priority of their policy concerns.

Most of the people engaged in policy work, though, are not leaders, but officials – mostly of government, but also of non-governmental organizations. Since the authoritative leaders are seen as the decision-makers, the other people in government who are doing policy work must be 'advisers' to these decision-makers, and the work they do is often called 'policy advising' (even if they have no contact with the leader whom they are 'advising') (Radin 2000). There has been a steady growth in policy-specific officials over the past couple of decades, particularly in the United States, where graduate courses in 'policy analysis' are common. These officials may be called 'policy analysts' or 'policy officers' and be located in a policy branch, or they may be less conspicuous as part of the management of the agency. They find themselves engaged in a range of activities – not simply the identification and comparison of options, as in classical 'policy analysis', but also negotiation with other participants (including responding to their initiatives), drafting, and the public presentation of policy. The attribute most commonly sought in advertisements for jobs of this sort is superior communication skills. These people are, in a sense, managing the 'collective puzzling' that Heclo (1974) identified, but this is described as 'policy advising'.

The other main group of policy participants outside government is bodies concerned with the governing of some area of practice: organizations of farmers, for instance, or hospital managers. As we saw in the previous chapter, these can be integral parts of the process of policy development, but in the authoritative choice account, they are seen as interested parties, seeking to influence the legitimate decision-maker. As policy positions and organizations became more common in government, non-governmental bodies tended to appoint policy staff of their own to facilitate their dealings with government. They tended to develop good working relations with their counterparts in government and other relevant bodies, and it was these networked relationships which were tagged by observers 'policy communities' (Richardson and Jordan 1979). In the authoritative choice account, this label was always slightly suspect since officials should not have close ties with 'outside interests', and sometimes, political leaders or top managers try to break up these 'cosy relationships'.

Just as the authoritative choice account identifies the participants in a particular ways, it also shapes the way we see the action. It sees policy activity as being about the making of decisions, which makes particular sorts of practice appropriate and legitimate. It has the effect of channelling activity towards a decision point, generating procedures and giving rise to presentations of government activity as the outcome of decisions. Operating agencies learn to present their operating as structured patterns of action, formally expressed and approved at some level ('policies'), and need to think in terms of the extent to which they need to formalize their operations and seek this sort of approval. They also find themselves extensively occupied in responding to policy initiatives from other agencies. Noordegraaf (2000a, b) found that policy managers lived a life of 'meetings and papers', as they coped with the demands of their own initiatives and their response to the initiatives of others. In this crowded and complex world, guardians of policy procedure emerge, such as the policy branch within the agency, or the cabinet secretariat, and try to impose order, defining when policy approval is required and in what form it should be sought, who needs to be consulted and whose approval is necessary. In many cases, particularly in government, formal procedures have emerged which appear to follow a model of rational choice: policy is made by an authorized decision, and decisions follow written submissions, which have to be made in specified ways at particular times. There may be rules for soliciting comments or (especially in the case of the legislature) provision for debate. These procedures are in the custody of specialist officials, such as the staff of the Cabinet Office, who use procedure to routinize the competition for resources. Agencies have to 'learn the ropes' of inter-organizational action, and policy workers often report that their training had not prepared them for this (see Adams 2005).

Framing the policy process in this way also offers a way of presenting and evaluating government. Candidates for public office are expected to declare policies on a wide range of issues, and the outcome of the election is held to be a popular endorsement of the policies of the winners: it is said to give them a mandate to implement these policies. Leaders describe the work of government in terms of the implementation of their policies, and policy activity as a way of demonstrating their leadership. When Gordon Brown finally became the British prime minister, his colleagues felt that he was not giving leadership, and his political support evaporated. 'We all thought Gordon was a brilliant policy guru, fizzing with ideas,' one cabinet member told me, 'but it turns out he isn't at all'. (Sylvester 2008).

Structured interaction

The authoritative choice account tends to assume the existence of a clear source of authority, but practitioners find that there are many voices in the air, some of them claiming some form of public authority, and others which are not part of government but which are clearly relevant and which should be part of the problem-solving. Radin (2000) found that policy analysts were often puzzled to find that their work consisted not so much of advising the decision-makers in their own agency as of negotiating with policy analysts from other organizations in search of a mutually accept-able outcome. This is why we also need to use the *structured interaction* account. The various participants will have their char-acteristic perspectives on the policy field, and policy development may challenge the assumptions and working practices of the organizations involved. This calls for interaction between organi-zations, possibly organizational change, and it may mean admitting new organizations – i.e. representatives of user groups – to the negotiating table.

Of course, there is a close relationship here between the author-itative choice and the structured interaction accounts of 'doing policy': in practice, each tends to assume the other. The participants engaged in the structured interaction know that any agreement they may reach will probably need endorsement by leaders for it to take effect. And leaders being asked to make an authoritative choice want to know that it is an appropriate course and likely to be accepted by the participants involved. This is recognized to an extent in the authoritative choice framework as 'consultation', and a great deal is written on how this should be done. There are really two central themes in this literature: a managerial theme, which sees consultation is a strategic act by managers to generate support for policies already decided (e.g. Bishop and Davis 2002), and a democratic theme, which sees it in terms of entitlement, empower-ment and 'ownership' of the policy (e.g. Fischer 1993). Any particular exercise in consultation will reflect the tension between the two themes in its own way. And the two themes may not be completely opposed to one another. As we saw in the previous chapter, health authorities have been happy to engage non-governmental organizations representing the sick in the manage-ment of health facilities, and in one Australian state, the function of policing government regulations on the transport of livestock has been contracted out to a non-governmental organization which is the advocate of animal interests: the Royal Society for the Pre-vention of Cruelty to Animals.

In the structured interaction account, then, much policy activity consists of building up and sustaining working relationships among different organizations (or distinct units within the same organization), an activity which predominantly falls to middle-level officials who can be thought of as the maintenance staff of the policy process. These officials are apt to remark that the most important attribute for a policy worker is neither expertise nor authority, but patience: they spend their time trying to make the activities of the various participants compatible with one another, in situations where different authorities are operating and there is no agreement on the best answer. This involves a great deal of interaction among the interested parties, ranging from individual telephone calls and informal chat at semi-social occasions, to public meetings and formal negotiations. There are many organized forums for this interaction, ranging from permanent committees to ad hoc working parties, and recognized processes of consultation, e.g. inviting interested parties to comment on the drafts of statements or other official documents. The object of this activity is to communicate to the other participants the policy perspective of the organization, to discover what their perspective is, to identify where the positions of the participants are in conflict and to seek paths to agreement. This may focus on the preparation of a new policy statement or it may be concerned with the implications of existing policies, e.g. the implications for local health authorities of central government policies on appropriate care for ex-service personnel.

In the process, the participants draw on the expert knowledge they have (or have acquired) of the policy subject matter – education, agriculture, forestry, etc. But they also draw on their detailed knowledge of the policy field: what has been done previously, which participants are involved, what they consider to be the important questions, what stances they have taken on key issues in the past, what commitments limit their freedom of action now, and so on. This knowledge helps them to find ways to knit together the diverse activities in a way which the different participants can accept. In this respect, 'making policy' is more like diplomacy than engineering.

It is at this level that 'outsiders' (i.e. not public officials) are most likely to engage in policy activity. Organizations emerge to represent a range of interests: in education policy, for instance, there are bodies to represent parents, teachers, disciplinary fields, employers, educators, and a variety of groups wanting to see their particular concerns – foreign languages, citizenship, international affairs, driving, drugs – better reflected in the curriculum. The policy process tends to draw organized interests into a stable relationship with the official players through recognized processes of consultation, and officials facilitate the recognition of representative groups: in this way, they organize their clientele. In doing this, they shape the way the policy question is understood and the interests that are recognized: some interests are organized in, and some are organized out.

The interest representatives themselves generally want to be on the inside, but once they get there, they are faced with a tension between asserting the viewpoint of their constituents and becoming involved in the detail of the policy process. Their claim to a place in the action is based on their knowledge of what their constituents want, but in the policy process these wants have to be related to all the other relevant factors, and the representatives may become involved in trading off the demands of their own constituents in the search for an agreed outcome.

Over time, the participants are drawn into the game, and both officials and the representatives of organized interests are engaged in the same sort of activity: an informed search for a workable and acceptable outcome. Representation becomes institutionalized and professionalized. Initially, it will be done by enthusiastic amateurs; as the organization becomes established, it engages paid, expert staff, who can be more effective in the detail work. The homelessness action group hires staff with qualifications in sociology and economics, who can talk to the policy professionals on their own terms. Governments facilitate the process by encouraging (often subsidizing) the formation of peak organizations, which both brings together small groups into one organization and raises the level of professional expertise in interest representation. Policy activity is concentrated on the negotiations among a knowledgeable group, 'camped permanently around each source of problems', as Davies (1964) put it, who share both a field of concern and a body of expert knowledge about it. This is a potential source of conflict with these interest organizations, a structural tension between authenticity and effectiveness: only the members can say how they really feel, but hiring the experts will give them a more effective voice in policy.

Social construction

This detailed, expert negotiation draws on, and reinforces, the shared body of policy knowledge, and here we can see the link between the structured interaction account and that of *social construction*: it is through the interactions that the social construction is developed and shared (or not: marginal voices are left out of the interaction, and their construction of the problem is unlikely to be taken seriously). In Australian agricultural policy, for instance, there are academics in fields such as agricultural science, plant biology and agricultural economics. There are also agricultural experts working for banks, trading companies, professional bodies and consulting firms, or as private consultants. There are journalists working for the press and for specialist industry-oriented journals. All of them are part of a specialist discourse about agriculture, and potential participants in the discussion of agricultural policy. They may have no formal standing in the process but their contribution can be important, particularly in the medium to long term, as the terms of the policy debate shift. Such changes often reflect changes in the environment, but they also stem from changes in the terms of the debate among the knowledge workers, which in turn reflects debate in the broader society. For instance, in the 1980s, the discourse on agricultural policy in Australia shifted from an assumption that, ultimately, farming should be protected, to an assumption that, essentially, market forces should operate, and this shift (which reflected the broader debate about the role of the state) could also be seen in the positions taken by organized interests in the industry. This debate was carried in a range of locations, public and less public, but over time there was a 'paradigm shift' – a fundamental change in the basic understandings on which policy rested, so that when, for instance, the tightly protected urban milk markets were deregulated, there was little public controversy.

We can see here the way in which policy work can be concerned with the social construction of the problem, but it is rarely so obvious. Participants may not be particularly conscious of the extent to which the discourse which they use defines the problem (and excludes other definitions); it may appear simply to be the obvious way to see the problem from their institutional position (see Hall 1993). Policy workers with a reform agenda are more likely to be conscious of this aspect of policy construction. One, a feminist in an education agency, described her role as 'counterhegemonic', that is, 'it is about problematising the status quo such that what is understood as normal becomes problematic' (Gill and Colebatch 2006: 255).

One of the most obvious ways for policy workers to shape the social construction of a policy question is through the standard North American style of policy analysis: the identification and comparison of options. There is a large literature which seeks to establish an 'expertise of choice', grounded in microeconomics. In essence, this is a utilitarian calculus: state the objective of the policy, identify alternative ways of pursuing this, estimate the likely costs and benefits of each and work out the most cost-effective option. More complex versions seek to identify the benefits for each of the affected parties, or to build in estimates of the 'implementability' of the proposal. This form of policy activity is well established, particularly in the United States. Many policy workers, however, would argue that this sort of analysis is not conclusive in itself (see Radin 2000), but can be if it helps to shape the terms of the debate among the participants – what is regarded as normal, what is a problem, how we know that it is a problem, and what possible responses there are – but its importance lies in the way in which it can be used in this continuing process: the analysis will not settle the question on its own. Tao (2006) finds that policy workers in US local government – leaders and officials – use policy analysis strategically in defence of their own agendas. The question for the policy workers is whether they seek to use policy analysis to shape public opinion or only for advising leaders. Bardach (2000) argued that the policy analyst should build support for his/her analysis among key stakeholders (but not the public). However, when Professor Garnaut completed his inquiry on Australian climate change policy in 2008, he did not simply present a report to the Australian government (authoritative choice), but also embarked on a series of town hall meetings to sell it to the public (social construction). But this led to criticism that he had not consulted key stakeholders (structured interaction), as Bardach would have suggested, but was acting as an advocate of his preferred course of action (Warren 2008).

One way in which policy workers may seek to have an impact on the social construction of a policy issue is to commission a public inquiry. This can be a way of ventilating the subject of concern, drawing out not only the usual participants but also the marginal players and those without an organizational base (see Degeling *et al.* 1993). These inquiries may emerge from the legislature (linking the authoritative choice and the social construction accounts). Holland argues that public inquiries held by the Australian parliament

> allow committee members to test and weigh up competing policy claims. Much of this testing is between competing arguments of different policy professionals, often different industry lobby groups (unions versus employers, for example). Inquiries are thus deliberative, canvassing and comparing policy options, but also critical, deliberately testing out the appropriateness of current government policies, searching for areas of potential change.
>
> (Holland 2006: 81)

The social construction of an issue also reflects the way in which it is measured, and policy work is often focused on this, through the collection of data and, in particular, the construction of technologies of measurement which will facilitate a change in the perception of what is acceptable. The oldest of these measurements, cost-benefit analysis, was first developed by the US Army Corps of Engineers to help them manage partisan demands from legislators. More recently, workers in health policy have started to use the 'disability-adjusted life year', which measures the impact of medical treatment on the health and longevity of the patient, and, by relating this data to the cost of treatment, challenging the decision autonomy of hospital clinicians.

Policy work is concerned with the maintenance of, or challenge to, the social construction of the policy issue. Majone (1989) saw policy analysis as more like the work of a courtroom lawyer than of a laboratory scientist: as finding good reasons for doing something. Roe (1994) argued that a critical aspect of policy development was the development of an overarching narrative – the 'story-line'. Nor is this simply an academic concept. In the press office of UK prime minister Tony Blair, there was a Head of Story Development – a policy worker whose job it was to make sure that what was being said by government added up to a good story. Policy work, then, has to do with making meaning, and, in particular, with managing a variety of meanings. Different participants will view both the problem and possible responses to it in their own ways, and policy workers will find themselves engaged in constructing an account which will be acceptable to a diversity of perspectives. This is likely to result in ambiguity and 'equifinal agreement' (we agree on what to do but not on why we are going to do it) (Donnellon *et al.* 1986).

Lessons for the policy practitioner

This discussion may leave the policy worker rather bewildered: the practice of policy work is complex, and we learn different things about it by using different accounts. The remainder of this section summarizes the main lessons.

Focus on policy as a field of activity rather than on 'policy-making'

We have avoided the familiar term 'policy-making' and talked instead of 'policy activity' because it is clear that there is a great deal of activity, and that it is not well described as policy-*making*. Some participants may be trying to create policy on an identified subject; others may be trying to prevent it, or, more likely, seeking to use the opportunity to advance their own agendas. It is difficult to identify one authority figure as the 'policy-maker', because this person is one of a number of participants, and many of these are responsible to other authority figures, so 'what the government wants' becomes problematic: the question becomes 'how do people produce the outcomes which are described as the decisions of the government?' And many of the participants are in any case not part of government in any formal sense. 'Non-officials' are active at putting matters on policy agendas, framing the problem, canvassing solutions and giving effect to the outcome. Environmental policy, for instance, reflects not so much the intentions of the government in relation to the environment as the success of environmental activists and others at making this an issue on which governments have to take a stance, mobilizing public opinion and electoral support, and establishing the terms of the debate. But their activities would rarely be described – by themselves or by observers – as 'making policy'. Talking about policy activity directs our attention first to the process, and only secondly to the outcome, particularly when the outcome is seen as a formal statement. Much policy work is only distantly connected to authorized statements about goals: it is concerned with relating the activities of different bodies to one another, with stabilizing practice and expectations across organizations and with responding to challenge, contest and uncertainty.

It may be that statements by authorized leaders about goals are brought into play, but there will be a great deal of other activity as well, and it is important that the terms we use do not give an undue prominence to one part of the game.

Policy activity is skilled, interactive practice

We can see that 'policy' is a particular perspective on the activities of government (and other organizations), and a policy approach is a distinctive practice that participants have to learn – and they learn it mostly through interaction with other participants. They learn ways of talking about issues which 'make sense' to other participants, and the sorts of evidence and arguments that will make their own concerns meaningful and valid, and will facilitate their continuing constructive place in the action. This does not mean that their claims will be accepted, but rather that both the claims and the people who make them will be taken seriously in the policy process. This process of 'normalizing' policy discussion is helped both by organizing by officials (e.g. formal processes of consultation) and by an increasing professionalization of policy activity, as governmental and non-governmental organizations create policy-specific positions and organizational segments, and use these to facilitate interaction between stakeholders on policy questions.

The policy literature may not give much guidance

Although there is a great deal of academic writing on the policy process, not much of it is concerned with what policy workers do, and what there is may not seem very useful to the harassed policy worker. Certainly, there are many 'standard economics-based policy analysis texts' (as one reviewer put it) produced for the North American market; the question is how the prescriptions in these texts relate to their experience of policy practice. Radin (2000: 183) finds that US policy analysts experience a 'disconnect' between the methodology of policy analysis that they have been taught in graduate school and the requirements of the policy work. This is partly because the academic writers tend to find the detail of policy practice 'messy' or 'chaotic', partly because, often, they are not particularly interested in just how their text relates to practice. Even Bridgman and Davis (2004), who entitle their text a 'handbook' for policy practitioners, describe it, at different points, as an empirical account (e.g. 'Australian experience suggests that a policy cycle is likely to begin with issue identification', p. 26), normative ('A policy cycle is something of an ideal – worth striving for if not always attainable', p. 2), heuristic ('A policy cycle is just a heuristic, an ideal type from which every reality will curve away', p. 100), and instrumental ('A policy process that does not include everything from problem identification to implementation has less chance of success', p. 24). They reach the conclusion that their text is a blend of all of them ('not quite descriptive, not confidentially normative, just an action plan for would-be policy-makers', p. 102), but Adams recounts that Australian policy workers who come to the job with an awareness of the Bridgman and Davis model of policy as systematic choice find that they are operating in a world 'constituted not by order and rationality but by uncertainty, interpretation, contested meanings, power, volatility, compressed views of time and space and partial information' (Adams 2005: 103).

Policy work involves choice

Policy is complex because you cannot attend to everything equally at the same time, and the participants have to respond to the competing demands on them in their own ways. Leaders, for instance, will have their own programme concerns, but they are also responsible for the continuing programmes of their agency, as well as the place of their agency in the constant jostling for influence. They are also concerned about the maintenance of electoral support, and about the struggle for influence within the leadership. Some may have their eyes fixed firmly on the programme on which they were elected. Others will be more interested in the continuing programmes of the agency and current challenges. Other leaders may be more interested in the process: 'How are we doing in the opinion polls?, Will we win the next election?, Are we maintaining our influence relative to other agencies?' No leader can completely ignore any aspect, but leaders will respond to this tension in different ways, reflecting their own experience and characteristics, recent policy history and the nature of the interest in this policy field.

Officials engaged in policy work have a different pattern of competing demands. When they have come to policy work from some field of professional practice (education, agriculture, forestry, etc.), they will be guided by their professional knowledge. But they will also be conscious of the history of the policy field: what has been done previously, which participants are involved, what they consider to be the important questions, what stances they have taken on key issues in the past, what commitments limit their freedom of action now, etc. They also (to some extent) map out their own personal style. In a detailed study of the orientations of policy workers in one Dutch ministry, Hoppe and Jeliazkova (2006) found that they could identify five distinct styles of policy worker: the process director, the policy philosopher, the policy adviser, the neo-Weberian, and the expert adviser. What is seen as good policy work will reflect not only the formal requirements of the job and the contextual demands of the situation, but also the personal style that individuals and groups of workers see as appropriate.

Non-officials are faced with the tension between influence and autonomy: whether it is better to stay outside the official sphere and retain complete freedom of action, or to come inside and have more influence, but accept that there will be restraints on your freedom to demand and to criticize. Here, there may be a tension between leaders and followers. Leaders of non-governmental organizations will understand the official agenda and look for ways to maximize their influence, but their followers may well be so accustomed to protest that any form of compromise with government is unacceptable to the rank and file. In the Australian state of Tasmania, a compromise between environmentalist leaders and the logging industry collapsed because the environmentalist followers felt that any form of agreement with 'the enemy' could only mean that their leaders had 'sold out'.

Policy implementation needs three lenses

We have stressed that it is not helpful to see 'policy-making' and 'policy implementation' as separate activities, following one another in sequence, but that 'implementation' is part of the language in use in policy practice, and the policy practitioner has to deal with it. Here again, the three accounts give three different perspectives. Through the authoritative choice lens, the policy worker knows to be attentive to the public statements and specific commitments which have been made and which could be taken as indicators of achievement – establishing the office, promulgating the regulations, spending the money. Through the structured interaction lens, the policy worker will know that there are multiple participants whose cooperation is necessary for this policy to have an impact, but that they all have their own agendas, and the task is to construct a form of collaboration which is compatible with these multiple agendas and has the support of important stakeholders, and through continuing negotiation, to maintain this support. Through the social construction lens, the policy worker will see the need to generate and sustain (in the face of this diversity of agendas) a shared understanding of the concerns behind the policy, who the relevant participants are, and what are the criteria for success. The policy worker will realize that this means that 'implementation' is not a phase of policy which comes at the end of the process, but an awareness which pervades every part of it (see Forester 1987).

Policy is concerned with stability and change

Policy work is aimed at stabilizing practice, and also at changing it. On the one hand, policy acts as a conservative force. Both in the narrow sense of 'formal official statements' and in the broader sense of 'the structured commitment of important resources', policy constrains the actions of the participants. On the other hand, participants pursue policy activity as a way of changing practice, both in the narrow sense (feminists demand policy on equal employment opportunities, neo-liberals push for a national competition policy) and in the broad sense (environmentalists push for an environmental protection agency, welfare activists monitor and publicize the distributional impact of rural subsidy schemes).

Authority figures enunciate existing policy, but they also serve as a focal point for those pushing for change. The expertise of those running the existing policy structure may well be matched by the expert knowledge of those seeking changes, even more so now that local activists have quick and easy access, through the internet, to a global range of expert knowledge. The desire for stability makes policy participants amenable, in the interests of order, to the accommodation of dissident voices who are willing to use appropriate methods to argue their case. This means that well-organized activists often find that official structures are more permeable than might have been thought.

Policy work means making sense of practice

Policy workers find themselves doing a lot of things, but if there is an overarching theme, it is that they are making sense of the activity of governing – in different ways, and to different audiences. And policy can be 'sensible' in terms of any of the three characteristics of policy that we mentioned at the beginning (p.8): order (this is the way it is always done), authority (this been approved by the right people), and expertise (this is approved by those who know). It is not always clear how these characteristics can be established, and in any case, they may push in different directions, which makes the job of the policy worker particularly difficult – but this is perhaps a little easier to bear if the worker understands why it is so difficult.

Further reading

Perhaps surprisingly, not a great deal is written about what policy participants actually do. Sometimes the memoirs which leaders write offer valuable insights into the policy process, particularly into the structured interaction which lies behind the public announcements; Crossman (1975) is a good example of a politician's memoirs, and Edwards, a policy worker turned academic, analyses pieces of policy activity in which she was involved using both the public account and her own diaries (Edwards 2000). Radin (2000) offers an insightful account of the development of policy analysis as an occupation in the United States, and Weiss (1982, 1991) is very helpful on how policy analysis is used. There are two excellent studies of policy workers in the Netherlands: Noordegraaf's work (2000a, b) on policy managers, and Hoppe and Jeliazkova (2006) on middle-level policy workers. Colebatch (2006a) discusses the nature of policy work and the accounts that are given of it, and Colebatch (2006b) brings together a number of studies of policy work in different countries. Yanow (1996) offers an interesting case study of the way that policy workers contribute to the social construction of policy, and the cases in Hajer and Wagenaar (2003) are accompanied by useful discussion.

9

Where Do We Go from Here?

Where have we been?

This book has explored the concept of policy in the process of governing – both as an analysis of the process and as a part of the process – as something which the participants themselves use to make sense of the world and to contribute to the action. And in a way, it has been a dialogue with what might be called a common-sense model which sees policy as 'what governments decide to do', and good policy as being about governments choosing the right goals, and pursuing them with the right instruments. In the course of this dialogue, it has become clear that there is a considerable divergence between this model of the policy process and the experience of the participants.

We saw that it is often difficult to make sense of the action as governments choosing and pursuing goals. Goals are hard to discern, ambiguous or conflicting; much of the action does not seem to have much to do with goals. Nor does it appear that the actors are 'governments'. In any policy field, there will be a wide range of interested parties – governmental, semi-governmental and not governmental at all – who will be involved for different reasons and who see the question in different ways. Any policy question is likely to involve a number of organizations, with differing understandings of the question and varying degrees of interest in cooperating with other bodies.

People (participants and observers) have responded to this divergence between the map of policy and the experience in different ways.

A reform agenda

For some, the divergence between the map and the practice gives rise to a reform agenda: the goal of reform should be to make well-informed choice the practice, and not just a theoretical propositional. Stone (1988) calls this 'the rationality project': the mission 'of rescuing public policy from the irrationalities and indignities of politics, hoping to conduct it instead with rational, analytical and scientific methods' (p. 4). This is a sentiment which underlies much of the enthusiasm for policy and policy units and policy analysis: if systematic analysis could be brought to bear on the problem, the most efficient course of action would be evident, and because it had emerged from this analysis, it would clearly be the right thing to do.

In this context, the focus on policy is a reform move: paying attention to outcomes rather than process, and making choices in order to accomplish priority goals rather than because of habit, political pressure or technological inertia. It was hoped that central policy review agencies in government, not being committed to existing programmes, would be better placed to review their contribution to the achievement of policy goals, and similar hopes were held of policy units in functional departments.

This systematic linking of policy choices, programmes and outcomes was, it was felt, particularly needed in government, which did not have the discipline of the 'bottom line' which was seen as central in business. A policy orientation would give a clear focus on outcomes, and public organization would clearly be an instrument for the accomplishment of policy objectives.

> The use of the term 'program' reflects the value now placed on the coherent organization of government activities into 'programs' of closely related components all of which are, or ought to be, managed according to the policy priorities established under the formal authority of the program objectives ... evaluation is the current phase of that deliberate pursuit of rational public management which originated in the struggles for program budgeting and management by objectives.
>
> (Uhr and Mackay 1992: 433)

Theory and practice

Another common response, especially among practitioners keen to assert that academics do not understand the 'real world', is to describe the model of policy as the pursuit of objectives as 'theory' and the more complex and puzzling experience as 'practice'. For example, 'in theory, policy is made by government making a clear choice of the most effective response to a known problem, but in practice it emerges from struggles between powerful interests pursuing different agendas and is marked by contest and uncertainty'. Here, 'theory' is being used not in the sense of an abstract explanation of the way the world works, but in a more normative way: this is the way that the world should work, but does not. In an ideal world, governments would single-mindedly begin with the problem and work out the best solution, but in practice there are many voices in government, and they all view the problem from the perspective of what they are doing themselves, and how to turn the policy-making to their advantage. The model of policy as the systematic pursuit of authorized objectives is seen as an ideal which people respect but are not necessarily expected always to follow.

The approach which we have been taking does not make a sharp distinction between 'theory' and 'practice', but recognizes that there are different accounts of the policy process, and that practitioners and observers will use them in different ways. Observers using an account of authoritative choice are likely to find the policy workers' knowledge of policy practice – about position and negotiation and compromise and commitment – difficult to accommodate. At best, it may help in facilitating the implementation of a decision made on other grounds. Policy practitioners need to work in a number of accounts. They need to be familiar with the procedures and rhetoric of authoritative choice: the decision procedures, the systematic study of needs, the ordering of options, the calculation of costs and benefits, etc. But they also need to be adept at structured interaction, being able to identify and collaborate with other participants, and to recognize the extent to which dealing with a policy is an exercise in social construction, and to be able to develop a shared discourse through which they can negotiate outcomes with other participants. Their difficulty is often that the literature and their academic training have not prepared them for this relationship between knowledge and practice.

An analytical tool

For some writers, the divergence between the two perspectives is not a problem. Analytical constructs in the social sciences, they would argue, are not descriptions of empirical cases, and differences between models and practice are neither surprising nor disturbing. For such writers, the development of a model of policy as authorized choice can help us to understand the policy process, even though the process does not resemble the model. Howlett and Ramesh (1995), for instance, develop a model of policy as a cycle of applied problem-solving: it begins with agenda-setting, which leads to policy formulation, then decision-making, policy implementation, and finally policy evaluation. They argue that 'this facilitates the understanding of public policymaking by breaking the complexity of the process into a limited number of stages and substages'.

Howlett and Ramesh stress, though, that the practice of policy does not follow the model. Decision-makers do not act in a systematic way, the stages may occur in a different order or be omitted entirely, there may be a series of small loops rather than one big one – 'In short, there is often no linear progression as conceived by the model' (Howlett and Ramesh 1995: 12). But although the model bears little resemblance to the experience of policy, they assert that if the model is further developed by being made more elaborate – i.e. by the development of a taxonomy of policy styles – 'such a model contributes to the development of a policy science by providing a much better understanding of why governments chose to do what they do or do not do' (p. 14). It is not clear, though, in what way a model which diverges so markedly from practice can offer a better understanding of practice.

A process of organizing

The argument in this book has been that policy emerges from the activity of organizing a complex world. There are many participants, differing understandings of the problem, and a variety of organizational locations and relationships through which action can be taken. In this challenging world, the participants constitute 'policy' and mobilize a number of different accounts of the process.

The first of these accounts presents policy as a process of authoritative choice: as Dye (1985) and others would put it, 'policy is what governments decide to do'. This focuses attention on 'the authorities', and defines their activity as 'making policy'. It also defines the activities of the other participants: they are engaged in either 'policy advice' (before the event) or 'policy implementation' (after it). Lines of authority are important in the vertical dimension: 'policy' is an assertion of authority over practice, limiting the autonomy of both officials and clients. It is important that officials be independent of outside influences and not be 'captured', e.g. that those concerned with environmental policy should end up as the voice of environmental interests within the government, rather than the instrument of the government. This account directs attention to goals, it acts as an inducement to organizations to enunciate objectives and to attach weight to them, e.g. by linking the pay of senior staff to the accomplishment of defined objectives.

A rather different account focuses on policy as structured inter-action. It does not assume a single decision-maker addressing a clear policy problem. It focuses instead on the range of participants in the game, the diversity of their understandings of the situation and the problem, the ways in which they interact with one another and the outcomes of this interaction. It does not assume that this pattern of activity is a collective effort to achieve known and shared goals. In this perspective, the policy process is a pattern of inter-action between participants engaged in different projects, rather than the pursuit of clear and shared objectives. The interaction will not be random, as the policy process operates to turn conflict and participation into routinized activities.

A third account, however, focuses on the way that policy activity reflects a pattern of shared meaning and how policy is socially constructed. Which situations demand action, who should be heard on these matters, and what course of action is appropriate, are matters emerging from collective discussion. Different participants are likely to have different answers to these questions, and one of the tasks for policy activity is to generate understandings which enable the various participant to collaborate with one another. An important dimension of this social construction is presenting the activity as official problem-solving, i.e. authoritative choice. Framing the process as problem-solving through authoritative choice is an important part of making the outcome acceptable: policy has force because it has been generated in a proper way. We live in a secular industrial society which believes in technology and rationality, and it calls for a technology of rational choice. As March and Olsen (1989: 52) put it: 'It is hard to imagine a society with modern Western ideology that would not require a well-elaborated and reinforced myth of intentional choice through politics, both to sustain a semblance of social orderliness and meaning and to facilitate change.' So the vertical perspective, in which policy is presented in terms of the pursuit of authorized goals, becomes an essential part of its validity: 'The ritual of identifying what their goals are and discussing them at the annual meeting was conveying to members and stakeholders that the organization is a modern, rational organization and that it is doing its work properly, even if it is difficult to demonstrate accomplishment of these goals' (Yanow 1996: 201).

These three accounts highlight different aspects of the policy process, and frame the action in divergent ways, and practitioners have to include all three in their practical knowledge. Officials know that even though their minister may have the legitimate authority to make policy decisions in a given area, those decisions will be more effective if they have emerged from continuing negotiation with the stakeholders, and are couched in terms of understandings which are shared among the stakeholders and command support from the public. Policy practitioners learn to present their activities in the appropriate account. Public recognition of the part that non-governmental stakeholders play in generating policy might be seen as a reduction of the significance of authorized leaders, and policy practitioners are careful to describe their involvement as 'consultation' leading to 'advice' and a subsequent 'decision'. These verbal forms make it possible for stakeholders to negotiate policy change in a way that can be presented as an authoritative decision.

This means that there is an element of ambiguity about policy-making, because the way in which accounts are used is itself part of the process. An outcome which has been negotiated among interested parties is set in place by being announced by the voice of authority: the minister, the board of directors, the national council. The production of this policy outcome is the work of many participants, but it is publicly presented as a choice by one point of authority. Having been constructed, it must be, as Weick (1979) puts it, 'enacted': the form of the presentation is part of the process. 'Everyone knows' that what is announced as a ministerial decision probably reflects a complex process of inter-organizational negotiation more than it does the preferences of that particular minister, but it is inappropriate to point this out: this is part of the 'profane' knowledge of the participants, and is not to be stated in the 'sacred' discourse of public announcements (see Colebatch and Degeling 1986). Authorized decision-making is an essential 'policy myth' in the sense described by Yanow: 'a narrative created and believed by a group of people which diverts attention from a puzzling part of their reality' (Yanow 1996: 191).

Where are we now?

Policy has proved an elusive concept, perhaps partly because it is used by practitioners (for whom ambiguity about definitions can be useful) as much as it is by social scientists. A satisfactory definition would have to recognize the tension between the model and the way it is used, e.g. 'policy is a term used to refer to the structuring of collective action by the mobilization of a model of governing as authoritative decision-making'. This is an awkward approach to a definition, but it does focus attention on the essential elements.

Policy is a process as well as an artefact

In the 'common-sense' use of the term, policy is an artefact: a thing created by 'policy-makers'. We read, for instance, that 'the government has announced its new policy on equal employment opportunity'; some would insist that there must be not only a press statement but also a commitment of resources (money, people), perhaps even a statute which expresses the policy. We have argued that these examples of formal policy activity can be understood only in terms of process, a continuing pattern of events and understanding which is structured by a sense of authorized decision-making. For instance, a demand for a population policy is built on a shared perception of the possibility of the conscious use of governmental authority to change the population pattern. The policy process encompasses all the action which takes place around the possibility of this use of governmental authority to structure action, and policy statements – such as White Papers or ministerial speeches – are part of this process of structuring.

Some would argue that this turns the whole of the policy world into a blur: there are (they would argue) clear policies – the environmental policy, the industry protection policy, the competition policy – and they need to be distinguished from the ordinary process of government. Moreover, they have objectives – the vocational education policy aims to raise the skills level in the workforce, the child immunization policy aims to reduce the level of communicable diseases among children – and we can therefore ask whether they 'work'. This is certainly a valid perspective, but it is an incomplete one. These formally stated policies have to be understood in the context of other stated policies – e.g. on the loosening of regulatory controls over the organization of work – and of the broader factors that structure action, such as the level of knowledge in government about skill needs in the workforce and the existence of organized links between industry, workers, trainers and government. Statements are important, but they must be understood in context. And as we saw from the discussion of evaluation, whether a programme has 'worked' depends on how the question is framed and who is asked: that, too, is about process.

But if we are concerned with policy as process rather than simply as formal acts by authorized decision-makers, we have to ask if the structuring without reference to authorized decision-makers should also be considered policy. For instance, a school may set about defining a 'discipline policy', holding discussions with interested parties, exploring alternatives, drafting a code of practice; it then has a policy on discipline. But did it have one before, when teachers made their own decisions on discipline, perhaps subject to appeal to the collective professional judgement of their colleagues? Should that also be considered policy? In the structured interaction account, it probably would be: policy as 'this is the way we do things here'.

Policy is concerned with creating coherence in the face of continuing ambiguity and contest

The problem we have been grappling with is that the map seems to be clearer than the terrain to which it relates: there is a shared image of a clear process of decision-making, but the experience is of context, ambiguity and confusion. We have seen that generating policy is an interplay of authority, organization and meaning, and that this is a source of ambiguity and conflict. We have also seen that much policy activity is in response to this diffusion of organization and understanding: how do we generate concerted action when there is no single answer and little prospect of imposing one solution in the face of resistance?

This means that policy is a field that will always be marked by ambiguity and structural tension. There is structural tension between authoritative choice, structured interaction and social construction: for instance, between implementing the choices made by government, incorporating all the relevant participants (stakeholders), and having a very clear idea of what we are trying to achieve. The stakeholders may not be interested in collaborating if the government has already made all the choices, and the more stakeholders are brought in, the more diversity there will be in view of the nature of the policy problem and what is an appropriate response And there will be ambiguity arising from the different perspectives that the participants have, from the (often deliberately) imprecise language used to express them, and from the gap between the experience of the participant and the terms used to describe it.

This is the source of the frustration which analysts of policy often field, but it is also the source of the interest. It is because there are no fixed points that participants attempt to find a point of anchorage – which is what they mean by policy. And it is the source of the rhetorical devices which the participants use to reconcile their experience with the model, such as the coexistence of 'sacred' and 'profane' accounts of the same policy experience.

Policy is problematic and graduated rather than definitive and absolute

We come to the realization that to ask 'what is the policy on x?' is to ask the wrong question, because it pushes us to look for a state-ment, but does not necessarily tell us the significance of this policy statement (if there is one). What we want to know is 'what deter-mines how things are done?', and this means that we want the answers to a lot of other questions. If there is a policy statement, who enunciated it? What sort of people take notice of it, and in what contexts? Is it linked to the pattern of resource allocation? What other factors are at work? In what way, then, is the policy statement significant? The focus shifts from 'is there a policy, and if so, what is it?', to 'in what sense is there policy, and what impact does it have?' The term is not a scientific absolute, but a socially constructed variable.

Where do we go next?

Some readers may feel that this discussion has made the task of understanding policy, and of participating in it, harder rather than easier. We may have started with a relatively clear idea of policy as being about governments making decisions, and ended up with a much broader concern with how the process of governing is structured. We saw that 'government' consisted of a wide range of specialized components, often following divergent paths, and that in any case it is recognized that governing involves other organizational forms, both nationally (i.e. community groups, non-governmental organizations, business, religious and kinship groups) and internationally (whether official bodies such as the World Trade Organization or less official bodies such as Greenpeace or the 'epistemic community' of climate scientists). We found, too, that we could not think of policy development as simply the writing of a document, but that it involved a great deal of interaction and idea-formation, not all of it consciously directed towards 'policy-making'.

Some people would say that while these are interesting reflections, there is still work to be done. There are, they would say, officials with policy responsibilities: some people do have to write, for instance, the organization's policy on workplace safety, or a policy submission to go to cabinet, and they cannot stop to think about what policy means; they just have to get on with the job. While we may not accept that you have to stop thinking in order to get on with the job, it is clear that there may be one agenda for analysts of the policy process, and another for policy practitioners.

An agenda for analysis

Perhaps the first lesson for those analysing the policy process is the importance of using a combination of disciplinary approaches. Policy is a political process, an organizational process and a process of social learning, and, as we have seen, these processes interact with one another: what is learned reflects how the issue is organized, which is in turn related to the way that issues and people are recognized in the political world.

We can see, too, that it is important to see policy as part of practice, not as something forged elsewhere and then imposed from above. Policy is something that the participants use as part of their practice – to codify and justify practice, to contest and change practice, and to assert their right to shape practice. Some of these participants are officials and designated policy specialists; others are drawn into policy activity because of professional responsibilities or personal commitment. In any case, the focus for analysis needs to be on what people do in the construction of policy, how their practice is stabilized and given official recognition, and how it relates to the continuing work of governing. In particular, we need to ask what the 'professional' policy people are doing. We have seen that while a specialist skill in 'policy analysis' has been developed, practitioners find that what they need to do does not look much like the policy analysis in the book. We need to know more about what it is that they do, why they see this as the appropriate course of action, and what are the outcomes of particular sorts of professional practice.

The analyst will also be concerned with the development of meaning in the policy process, at two levels. At one level, what a policy question is 'about' is not given, but is likely to be the subject of dispute between participants with different perspectives and agendas, so a critical question is how a basis for action is constructed among these differing interpretations. How is the discourse managed and an 'order of discourse' constructed? At a deeper level, as we have seen, the concept of policy itself has a number of strands of meaning, including order, authority and understanding, and the analyst will be asking how exercises in governing are constructed as policy: what is it that the participants do that makes it 'policy'?

One of the greatest challenges for the analyst is the significance for policy of the argument that governing is now more diversified, with national governments sharing the work with local initiatives, non-governmental bodies, contractors and a range of international actors. The traditional framing of policy has assumed a personified 'decision-maker' who made choices in order to achieve a known outcome. What are the implications of recognizing that policy may be the outcome of interaction among a number of participants with different agendas? How is the instrumental rhetoric of authoritative choice used to structure action among such a diversity of participants?

An agenda for practice

Some of the academic writing on policy presents itself as a guide to practice, e.g. such books as *Policy Analysis for the Real World* (Hogwood and Gunn 1984) and *The Australian Policy Handbook* (Bridgman and Davis 2000, 2004). As we have noted, academic writing *about* the policy process can be mobilized *in* that process. Much of it is, as Stone (1988) put it, part of the 'rationality project', and is based on the conviction that policy *ought* to be generated by the model of rational decision-making depicted in the 'policy cycle' model. Authors writing from this perspective believe that policy would be better if it followed the 'stage' model: problem leads to investigation leads to solution. The authors may concede that it is just as likely to work the other way around – that demands for a particular course of action lead to an investigation which identifies a problem – but this is seen as deviant behaviour. This leads to tension between empirical observation and the tenets of the model.

> Ideally a government will have a well developed and widely distributed policy framework, setting out economic, social and environmental objectives. It will behave corporately, a unity with multiple parts in pursuit of the same goals.
> In practice, such overall policy frameworks are rarely documented cohesively.
>
> (Bridgman and Davis 2000: 91)

There is a strong normative element here: 'Coordination in government is a virtue', they say (Bridgman and Davis 2000: 90). This is, of course, part of the rationale of the central agency. Bridgman and Davis are former cabinet officials, and they have a particular interest in articulating a perspective on policy which validates the activities of central agencies, and which is supported by academic writing from within 'the rationality project'.

At the same time, there are policy workers and policy routines (such as cabinet procedures) which they have to follow. The question is how this sort of work is understood. Is it seen as 'the government moving to solve problems' or as 'people interacting to reorder social practice by mobilizing the idea of government'? If it is framed as 'government solving problems', then the 'stage' model makes sense: define the problem, identify alternative solutions and then consult with the stakeholders before reaching a final decision. But if it is more broadly framed, then the first question might be: 'How is this constituted as a problem? By whom? What other ways might there be of framing this question?' In the first framing, one might try to identify the common goal; as Bridgman and Davis (2000: 90) write: 'Policies are based on shared goals.' But in the second framing, one would recognize that not all players share the same goals (as Bridgman and Davis recognize: 'Departments and statutory authorities have their own goals and perspectives' (p. 91)) and that therefore the task is to negotiate a shared meaning among participants who do not have common goals.

So the first task for the practitioner would be not to identify the government's policy goals, but to analyse the policy situation being addressed, asking:

- How are matters constructed as policy issues? This would include identifying different ways of perceiving the question, and the extent to which these perceptions are identified with particular categories of people.
- What aspects of governing are under review? The question can be framed in diverse ways at different levels, and participants are likely to recognize different foci of action.
- Who can participate? That is, who is interested, who is affected, and to what extent are they organized and skilled in ways that facilitate their involvement in official processes? In particular, if policy is concerned with changing the understandings and practices of the unorganized, through what processes is this seen as happening, and where do those whose behaviour is to be changed come into the picture?
- What are the organizational locations in which the action will take place, and how are the rules of engagement determined? How will this affect the way in which the question is defined and the participants determined?
- How is policy activity as a process of scrutiny related to the continuing practices of 'ordinary governing'? How will any changes be felt? How might this be taken into account in the policy activity itself?
- What is the timeframe in which the various participants are working? Leaders want to see results quickly, even when the effects of policy changes may not be felt for decades. The people affected by the policy are likely to have much longer memories than officials who are always subject to transfer. And for all the participants, there is a relevant past, and a future – and it is likely that it will be different for each of them.

So our exploration of policy as a concept brings us to a set of questions about how the participants shape the action (and how non-participants come to be excluded), and the ideas on which they draw – not the least of which is the idea of 'policy' – and the organizational practices and underlying values on which these ideas rest, because, in the end, it is what policy participants do with the idea that determines what 'policy' means.

Bibliography

Adams, D. (2005) Review of P. Bridgman and G. Davis *The Australian Policy Handbook*, Sydney, Allen and Unwin, 3rd ed., 2004, *Australian Journal of Public Administration*, 62(1): 102–3.

AIHW (Australian Institute of Health and Welfare) (2007) *Health Expenditure Australia 2005–06*. Canberra: AIHW.

AIHW (Australian Institute of Health and Welfare) (2008) *Australia's Health 2008*. Canberra: AIHW.

Aldrich, H. E., Fowler, S. W., Liou, N. and Marsh, S. J. (1994) Other people's concepts: why and how we sustain historical continuity in our field, *Organization*, 1: 65–80.

Allison, G. T. (1971) *Essence of Decision*. Boston: Little, Brown.

Althaus, C., Bridgman, P. and Davis, G. (2008) *The Australian Policy Handbook*, 4th edn. Sydney: Allen & Unwin.

Anderson, G. (2006) Ministerial staff: new players in the policy game, in H. K. Colebatch (ed.) *Beyond the Policy Cycle: The Policy Process in Australia*, Sydney: Allen & Unwin, pp. 166-83.

Anderson, J. E. (1997) *Public Policymaking*, 3rd edn. Boston: Houghton Mifflin.

Anderson, J. E., Brady, D. W., Bullock, III, C. S. and Stewart, Jr., J. S. (1984) *Public Policy and Politics in America*. Montgomery, CA: Brooks/Cole.

Andrews, C. J. (2007) Rationality in policy decision-making. In F. Fischer, G. J. Miller and M. S. Sidney (eds) *Handbook of Public Policy Analysis*. Boca Raton, FL: CRC Press, pp. 161–72.

Atkinson, M. M. and Coleman, W. D. (1992) Policy communities, policy networks and the problems of governance, *Governance*, 5: 154–80.

Auer, M.R. (2006). The policy sciences in critical perspective. In J. Rabin, W. B. Hildreth and G. L. Miller (eds) *Handbook of Public Administration*. London: Taylor & Francis, pp. 545–62.

Ayres, I. and Braithwaite, J. (1992) *Responsive Regulation: Transcending the Deregulation Debate*. New York: Oxford University Press.

Bache, I. and Flinders M. (eds) (2004) *Multi-level Governance*. Oxford: Oxford University Press.

Ballard, J. A. (1989) The politics of AIDS. In H. Gardner (ed.) *Health Policy in Australia*. Melbourne: Churchill Livingstone.

Bang, H.P. (ed.) (2003) *Governance as Social and Political Communication*. Manchester: Manchester University Press.

Bardach, E. (1977) *The Implementation Game*. Cambridge, MA: MIT Press.

Bardach, E. (2000) *A Practical Guide for Policy Analysis: The Eightfold Path to More Effective Problem Solving*. New York: Chatham House.

Barrett, S. and Fudge, C. (1981) *Politics and Action*. London: Methuen.

Baume, P. (1995) Towards a health policy, *Australian Journal of Public Administration*, 54(1): 97–101.

Baumgartner, F. R. and Jones, B. D. (1991) Agenda dynamics and policy subsystems, *Journal of Politics*, 53: 1044–74.

Bemelmans-Videc, M-L., Rist, R.C. and Vedung, E. (1998), *Carrots, Sticks and Sermons: Policy Instruments and their Evaluation*. New Brunswick, NJ: Transaction Books.

Bennett, C.J. and Howlett, M. (1992) The lessons of learning: reconciling theories of policy learning and policy change, *Policy Sciences, 25(3)*: 275–94.

Benson, J. K. (1975) The interorganizational network as a political economy, *Administrative Science Quarterly*, 20: 229–49.

Benson, J. K. (1977) Organizations: a dialectical view, *Administrative Science Quarterly*, 22: 1–21.

Benson, J. K. (1982) A framework for policy analysis. In D. I. Rogers and D. Whetten (eds) *Interorganizational Coordination: Theory, Research and Implementation*. Ames: Iowa State University Press.

Berger, P. L. and Luckman, T. (1975) *The Social Construction of Reality: A Treatise on the Sociology of Knowledge*. Harmondsworth: Penguin.

Bevir, M., Rhodes, R.A.W. and Weller, P. (2003) Traditions of governance: interpreting the changing role of the public sector, *Public Administration, 81(1)*: 1–17.

Bishop, P. and Davis, G. (2002) Mapping public participation in policy choices, *Australian Journal of Public Administration 61(1)*: 14–29.

Bjorkman, J. W. and Altenstetter, C. (eds) (1998) *Health Policy*. Aldershot: Edward Elgar.

Bobrow, D. B. (2006) Policy design: ubiquitous, necessary and difficult. In B. G. Peters and J. Pierre (eds) *Handbook of Public Policy*. London: Sage, pp. 75–96.

Bogason, P. (2006) Networks and bargaining in policy analysis. In B. G. Peters and J. Pierre (eds) *Handbook of Public Policy*. London: Sage, pp. 97–115.

Borras, S. and Jacobsson, K. (2004) The open method of co-ordination and new governance patterns in the EU, *Journal of European Public Policy*, 11(2): 185–208.

Börzel, T. (1997) What's so special about policy networks? An exploration of the concept and its usefulness in studying European governance. *European Integration Online Papers* 1(16).

Börzel, T. A. (1998) Organizing Babylon: on the different conceptions of policy networks, *Public Administration*, 76(2): 253–73.

Bovens, M., t'Hart, P. and Kuipers, S. (2006) The politics of policy evaluation. In R.E. Goodin, M. Moran and M. Rein (eds) *The Oxford Handbook of Public Policy*, Oxford: Oxford University Press, pp. 319–35.

Boyer R. (1990) *The Regulation School: A Critical Introduction* (trans. C. Charney). New York: Columbia University Press.

Braybrooke, D. and Lindblom, C. E. (1963) *A Strategy of Decision*. New York: Free Press.

Bridgman, P. and Davis, G. (2000) *The Australian Policy Handbook*, 2nd edn. Sydney: Allen & Unwin.

Bridgman, P. and Davis, G. (2004) *The Australian Policy Handbook*, 3rd edn. Sydney: Allen & Unwin.

Burchell, G., Gordon, C. and Miller, P. (eds) (1991) *The Foucault Effect: Studies in Governmentality*. Hemel Hempstead: Harvester Wheatsheaf.

Cabinet Office (1999) *Professional Policy Making for the Twenty-First Century*. London: Cabinet Office.

Caiden, G. E. (1982) *Public Administration*, 2nd edn. Pacific Palisades, CA: Palisades Publishers.

Chouliaraki, L. and Fairclough, N. (1999) *Discourse in Late Modernity: Rethinking Critical Discourse Analysis*. Edinburgh: Edinburgh University Press.

Clemons, R.S. and McBeth, M. K. (2001) *Public Policy Praxis – Theory and Pragmatism: A Case Approach,* Upper Saddle River, NJ: Prentice Hall.

Cobb, R. W. and Elder, C. D. (1972) *Participation in American Politics: The Dynamics of Agenda-building*. Baltimore, MD: Johns Hopkins University Press.

Colebatch, H. K. (2002) Government and governmentality: using multiple approaches to the analysis of government, *Australian Journal of Political Science,* 37(3): 417–35.

Colebatch, H. K. (2006a) Policy, models and the construction of governing, in H. K. Colebatch (ed.) *The Work of Policy: An International Survey*. Lanham, MD: Lexington Books, pp. 3–19.

Colebatch, H. K. (ed.) (2006b) *The Work of Policy: An International Survey*. Lanham, MD, Lexington Books.

Colebatch, H. K. (ed.) (2006c) *Beyond the Policy Cycle: The Policy Process in Australia*. Sydney: Allen & Unwin.

Colebatch, H. K. and Degeling, P. (1986) Talking and doing in the work of administration, *Public Administration and Development*, 6: 339–56.

Coleman, W. D. and Skogstad, G. (1990) Policy communities and policy networks: a structural approach. In W. D. Coleman and G. Skogstad (eds) *Policy Communities and Public Policy in Canada*. Mississauga, ON: Copp Clark Pitman.

Commonwealth of Australia (1994) *Better Health Outcomes for Australians*. Canberra: AGPS.

Commonwealth of Australia (1997) *Climate Change: Australia's Second National Report under the United Nations Framework Convention on Climate Change*. Canberra: Department of the Environment.

Commonwealth of Australia (2008) *Garnaut Climate Change Review 2008*, Draft Report. Canberra: Australian Government.

Crenson, M. A. (1971) *The Unpolitics of Air Pollution: A Study of Non-decisionmaking in the Cities*. Baltimore, MD: Johns Hopkins University Press.

Crossman, R. (1975) *The Diaries of a Cabinet Minister*. London: Hamilton Cape.

Cuthbertson, G. M. (1975) *Political Myth and Epic*. East Lansing, MI: Michigan State University Press.

Davies, A. F. (1964) *Australian Democracy*. Melbourne: Cheshire.

Davies, H. T. O., Nutley, S. M. and Smith, P. C. (eds) (2000) *What Works? Evidence-based Policy and Practice in Public Services*. Bristol: Policy Press.

Davies, P. (2004) Is evidence-based policy possible? The Jerry Lee Lecture, Campbell Collaboration Colloquium, Washington, DC.

Dean, M. (1995) Governing the unemployed self in an active society, *Economy and Society*, 24(4): 559–83.

Dean, M. (1999) *Governmentality: Power and Rule in Western Society*. London: Sage.

Dean, M. and Hindess, B. (eds) (1998) *Governing Australia*. Cambridge: Cambridge University Press.

Dearlove, J. (1973) *The Politics of Policy in Local Government*. Cambridge: Cambridge University Press.

Degeling, P. (2001) Re-making policy in health. Paper presented to the Public Policy Network Conference, University of New South Wales, February.

Degeling, P., Baume, P. and Jones, K. (1993) Staging an official inquiry for policy change: the case of the Drug Evaluation Review in Australia, *Policy and Politics*, 21: 259–74.

De La Porte, C. (2001) Social benchmarking, policy making and new governance in the EU, *Journal of European Social Policy*, 11(4): 291–307.

DiMaggio, P. and Powell, W. W. (1991) The iron cage revisited: institutional isomorphism and collective rationality in organizational fields. In W. W. Powell and P. DiMaggio (eds) *The New Institutionalism in Organizational Analysis*. Chicago, IL: University of Chicago Press.

Dobbin, F. (1994) *Forging Industrial Policy: The United States, Britain and France in the Railway Age*. Cambridge: Cambridge University Press.

Donnellon, A., Gray, B. and Bougon, M.C. (1986) Communication, meaning, and organized action, *Administrative Science Quarterly*, 31(1): 43–55.

Doornbos, M. (2001) 'Good Governance': the rise and decline of a policy metaphor? *Journal of Development Studies*, 37(6): 93–108.

Dowding, K. (1995) Model or metaphor: a critical review of the policy network approach, *Political Studies*, 43: 136–58.

Dowding, K. (2001) There must be end to confusion: policy networks, intellectual fatigue, and the need for political science methods courses in British universities, *Political Studies*, 49(1): 89–105.

Dror, Y. (1971) *Design for the Policy Sciences*. New York: Elsevier.

Dror, Y. (2006) Training for policy-makers. In R. E. Goodin. M. Moran and M. Rein (eds) *The Oxford Handbook of Public Policy*, Oxford: Oxford University Press, pp. 80–106.

Dryzek, J. S. (1990) *Discursive Democracy: Politics, Policy, and Political Science*. New York: Cambridge University Press.

Dudley, G. and Richardson, J. (1998) Arenas without rules and the policy change process: outsider groups and British roads policy, *Political Studies*, 46(4): 727–47.

Durning, D. (1993) Participatory policy analysis in a social service agency: a case study, *Journal of Policy Analysis and Management*, 12(2): 297–322.

Dye, T. R. (1972) *Understanding Public Policy*. Englewood Cliffs, NJ: Prentice Hall.

Dye, T. R. (1985) *Understanding Public Policy*, 5th edn. Englewood Cliffs, NJ: Prentice Hall.

Edelman, M. (1964) *The Symbolic Uses of Politics*. Urbana, IL: University of Illinois Press.

Edelman, M. (1971) *Politics as Symbolic Action*. New York: Academic Press.

Edelman, M. (1977) *Political Language: Words that Succeed and Policies that Fail*. New York: Institute for the Study of Poverty.

Edelman, M. (1988) *Constructing the Political Spectacle*. Chicago, IL: University of Chicago Press.

Edwards, M. (2000) *Social Policy, Public Policy: From Problem to Practice*. Sydney: Allen & Unwin.

Eisenstein, H. (1991) *Gender Shock: Practising Feminism on Two Continents*. Sydney: Allen & Unwin.

Ergas, H. (2008) Beware Green zealots, *The Australian*, 1 July.

Fairclough, N. (2001) *Language and Power*, 2nd edn. London, Pearson Education.

Fischer, F. (1993) Citizen participation and the democratization of policy expertise: from theoretical inquiry to practical cases, *Policy Sciences,* 26(3): 165–87.

Fischer, F. (2003) *Reframing Public Policy.* Oxford: Oxford University Press.

Fischer, F. and Forester, J. (eds) (1993) *The Argumentative Turn in Policy Analysis and Planning.* London: Duke University Press/UCL.

Fischer, F. and Hajer, M. (1999) *Living with Nature: Environmental Politics as Cultural Discourse.* Oxford: Oxford University Press.

Fischer, F., Miller, G. J. and Sidney, M. S. (2007) *Handbook of Public Policy Analysis: Theory, Politics and Methods.* Boca Raton, FL: CRC Press.

Forester, J. (1981) Questioning and organizing attention toward a critical theory of planning and administrative practice, *Administration and Society,* 13(2): 161–205.

Forester, J. (1987) Anticipating implementation: normative practices in planning and policy analysis, in F. Fischer and J. Forester (eds) *Confronting Values in Policy Analysis: The Politics of Criteria.* Newbury Park CA: Sage.

Forester, J. (1993) *Critical Theory Public Policy and Planning Practice.* Albany, NY: SUNY Press.

Forester, J. (1997) Beyond dialogue to transformative learning: how deliberative rituals encourage political judgment in community planning processes. In D. Borri, A. Khakee and C. Lacirignola (eds) *Evaluating Theory–Practice and Urban–Rural Interplay in Planning.* Dordrecht: Kluwer, pp. 81–103.

Foster, C. D. and Plowden, F. J. (1996) *The State Under Stress.* Buckingham: Open University Press.

Foucault, M. (1986) *History of Sexuality.* New York: Pantheon.

Freedland, J. (2007) Gore and peace, *Guardian,* 12 October.

Friedrich, C. J. (1963) *Man and His Government.* New York: McGraw-Hill.

Friedson, E. (1986) *Professional Powers: A Study of the Institutionalization of Formal Knowledge.* Chicago, IL: University of Chicago Press.

Fung, A. and Wright, E. O. (2003) *Deepening Democracy. Institutional Innovations in Empowered Participatory Governance. The Real Utopias Project 1V.* London: Verso.

Georgiou, P. (1973) The goal paradigm and notes toward a counter-paradigm, *Administrative Science Quarterly,* 18: 291–310.

Geuijen, K., Yesilkagit, K. and t'Hart, P. (2006) Of bureaucrat-diplomats and street-level entrepreneurs: differentiated civil service practices in European policy networks. Paper presented to the Interpretive Policy Analysis Conference, University of Birmingham, June 2006.

Giddens, A. (1984) *The Constitution of Society.* Cambridge: Polity Press.

Gill, Z. and Colebatch, H. K. (2006) 'Busy little workers': policy-makers' own accounts, in H. K. Colebatch (ed.) *Beyond the Policy Cycle: The Policy Process in Australia*. Sydney: Allen & Unwin, pp. 240–65.

Goodin. R.E., Moran, M. and Rein, M. (eds) (2006) *The Oxford Handbook of Public Policy*, Oxford: Oxford University Press.

Grant, W. and Peters, M. (2000) *Agricultural Policy*. Aldershot: Edward Elgar.

Gray, G. (2001) Taking care of voters, *The Australian*, 14 March, p. 10.

Gregory, R. (1989) Political rationality or 'incrementalism'? Charles E. Lindblom's enduring contribution to public policy making theory, *Policy and Politics*, 17: 139–53.

Griggs, S. (2007) Rational choice in public policy: the theory in critical perspective. In F. Fischer, G. J. Miller and M. S. Sidney (eds) *Handbook of Public Policy Analysis*. Boca Raton, FL: CRC Press, pp. 173–86.

Guba, E. G. and Lincoln, Y. S. (1989) *Fourth Generation Evaluation*. Newbury Park, CA: Sage.

Gunn, L. (1987) Perspectives on public management. In J. Kooiman and K. A. Eliassen (eds) *Managing Public Organisations*. London: Sage.

Gusfield, J. R. (1981) *The Culture of Public Problems*. Chicago, IL: University of Chicago Press.

Haas, P. M. (1992a) Introduction: epistemic communities and international policy coordination, *International Organisation*, 46(1): 1–35.

Haas, P. M. (1992b) Banning chlorofluorocarbons: epistemic community efforts to protect stratospheric ozone, *International Organization*, 46(1): 187–224.

Habermas, J. (1984) *The Theory of Communicative Action*. Vol. 1: *Reason and the Rationalization of Society*. Boston: Beacon Press.

Habermas, J. (1989) *The Structural Transformation of the Public Sphere: An Inquiry into a Categorization of Bourgeois Society*. Cambridge: Polity Press.

Hajer, M.A. (1995) *The Politics of Environmental Discourse: Ecological Modernization and the Policy Process*. New York: Oxford University Press.

Hajer, M.A. (2003a) A frame in the fields; policymaking and the reinvention of politics. In M.A. Hajer and H. Wagenaar (eds) *Deliberative Policy Analysis: Understanding Governance in the Network Society*. Cambridge: Cambridge University Press, pp. 88–110.

Hajer, M.A. (2003b) Policy without polity? Policy analysis and the institutional void, *Policy Sciences,* 36(2): 175–95.

Hajer, M.A. and Wagenaar, H. (eds) (2003) *Deliberative Policy Analysis: Understanding Governance in the Network Society*. Cambridge: Cambridge University Press.

Hale, D. (1988) Just what is a policy, anyway? And who's supposed to make it?, *Administration and Society*, 19: 423–52.

Hall, P. A. (1993) Policy paradigms, social learning and the state: the case of economic policymaking in Britain, *Comparative Politics*, 25(3): 275–96.

Halpin, D. (2002) Interest groups and (re-)establishing stability in policy making: the case of the NSW Farmers' Association and the Native Vegetation Conservation Act, *Australian Journal of Political Science,* 37(3): 489–507.

Ham, C. and Hill, M. (1984) *The Policy Process in the Modern Capitalist State*. Brighton: Wheatsheaf.

Healey, P. (1992) A planner's day: knowledge and action in communicative practice, *Journal of the American Planning Association*, 58(1): 9–20.

Healey, P. (1993) Planning through debate: the communicative turn in planning theory. In F. Fischer and J. Forester (eds) *The Argumentative Turn in Policy Analysis and Planning*. Durham, NC: Duke University Press, pp. 233–53.

Heclo, H. (1974) *Social Policy in Britain and Sweden*. New Haven, CT: Yale University Press.

Heclo, H. (1977) *A Government of Strangers: Executive Politics in Washington*. Washington, DC: Brookings Institution.

Heclo, H. (1978) Issue networks and the executive establishment. In A. King (ed.) *The New American Political System*. Washington, DC: American Enterprise Institute, pp. 87–124.

Heclo, H. and Wildavsky, A. (1974) *The Private Government of Public Money*. London: Macmillan.

Heidenheimer, A. J. (1986) *Politics, policy* and *police* as concepts in English and Continental languages: an attempt to explain divergences, *Review of Politics*, 48: 3–30.

Hendriks, F. (1999) *Public Policy and Political Institutions: The Role of Culture in Traffic Policy*. Aldershot: Edward Elgar.

Héritier, A. (1999) *Policy-making and Diversity in Europe: Escape from Deadlock*. Cambridge: Cambridge University Press.

Hill, M. (1997) Implementation theory: yesterday's issue? *Policy and Politics*, 25: 375–85.

Hill, M. and Hupe, P. (2002) *Implementing Public Policy: Governance in Theory and in Practice*. London: Sage.

Hisschemöller, M., Hoppe, R., Dunn, W. N. and Ravetz, J. R. (eds) (2001) *Knowledge, Power, and Participation in Environmental Policy Analysis*. Piscataway, NJ: Transaction Publishers.

Hodson, D. and Maher, I. (2001) The open method as a new mode of governance: the case of soft economic policy coordination, *Journal of Common Market Studies,* 39(4): 719–46.

Hogwood, B. W. and Gunn, L. A. (1984) *Policy Analysis for the Real World*. London: Oxford University Press.

Holland, I. (2002) *Accountability of Ministerial Staff?* Research Paper No.

19, 2001–02. Canberra: Department of the Parliamentary Library, Commonwealth of Australia.

Holland, I. (2006) Parliamentary committees as an arena for policy work. In H.K. Colebatch (ed.) *Beyond the Policy Cycle: The Policy Process in Australia.* Sydney: Allen & Unwin, pp. 66–90.

Hood, C.C. (1983) *The Tools of Government.* London: Macmillan.

Hood, C.C. (2006) The tools of government in the information age. In R. E. Goodin, M. Moran and M. Rein (eds) *The Oxford Handbook of Public Policy*, Oxford: Oxford University Press, pp. 469–81.

Hoppe, R. and Jeliazkova, M. (2006) How policy workers define their job: a Netherlands case study. In H. K. Colebatch (ed.) *The Work of Policy: An International Survey.* Lanham, MD, Lexington Books, pp. 35–60.

Howlett, M. and Ramesh, M. (1995) *Studying Public Policy.* Toronto: Oxford University Press.

Hughes, O. E. (1994) *Public Management and Administration.* London: Macmillan.

Jackson, P. M. (1988) The management of performance in the public sector, *Public Money and Management*, 10(4): 13–21.

Jackson, R. J. (1995) Foreign models and Aussie rules: executive–legislative relations in Australia, *Political Theory Newsletter*, 7: 1–18.

Jenkins, W. I. (1978) *Policy Analysis: A Political and Organisational Perspective.* London: Martin Robertson.

Jenkins-Smith, H. C. (1990) *Democratic Politics and Policy Analysis.* Pacific Grove, CA: Brooks/Cole.

Jones, B. D. (1994) *Reconceiving Decision-making in Democratic Politics: Attention, Choice, and Public Policy.* Chicago: University of Chicago Press.

Jones, B. D. and Baumgartner, F. R. (2005) *The Politics of Attention: How Government Prioritizes Problems.* Chicago: University of Chicago Press.

Jones, B. D., Boushey, G. and Workman, S. (2006) Behavioural rationality and the policy process: toward a new model of organizational information processing. In B. G. Peters and J. Pierre (eds) *Handbook of Public Policy*, London: Sage, pp. 49–74.

Jordan, A., Wurzel, R. K. W. and Zito, A. R. (eds) (2003) *'New' Instruments of Environmental Governance: National Experiences and Prospects.* London: Frank Cass.

Jung, K. (2002) Constitution and maintenance of feminist practice: a comparative case study of sexual assault centres in Australia and Korea, PhD thesis, University of New South Wales, Australia.

Kaufman, H. (1976) *Are Government Organizations Immortal ?* Washington, DC: Brookings Institution.

Keen, S. (2002) *Knowledge, Power and Democracy.* Sydney: Federation Press.

Kelly, M. and Maynard-Moody, S. (1993) Policy analysis in the post-positivist era: engaging stakeholders in evaluating the economic development districts program, *Public Administration Review,* 53(2): 135–42.

Kenis, P. and Schneider, V. (1991) Policy networks and policy analysis: scrutinising a new analytical toolbox. In B. Marin and R. Mayntz (eds) *Policy Networks: Empirical Evidence and Theoretical Considerations.* Boulder, CO/Frankfurt: Westview/Campus Verlag, pp. 25–62.

Kickert, W. J. M., Klein, E-H. and Koppenjan, J. F. M. (eds) (1997) *Managing Complex Networks: Strategies for the Public Sector.* London: Sage.

Kingdon, J. W. (1984) *Agendas, Alternatives and Public Policies.* Boston, MA: Little, Brown.

Kohler-Koch, B. and Eising, R. (eds) (1999) *The Transformation of Governance in the European Union.* London: Routledge.

Kooiman, J. (2003) *Governing as Governance.* London: Sage.

Kuhn, T. (1962) *The Structure of Scientific Revolutions.* Chicago, IL: University of Chicago Press.

Larner, W. and Walters, W. (eds) (2006) *Global Governmentality: Governing International Spaces.* London: Routledge.

Lasswell, H. D. (1936) *Politics: Who Gets What, When and How.* Cleveland, OH: Meridian Books.

Lasswell, H. D. (1951) The policy orientation. In D. Lerner and H. D. Lasswell (eds) *The Policy Sciences.* Stanford, CA: Stanford University Press.

Lasswell, H. D. and Kaplan, A. (1970) *Power and Society.* New Haven, CT: Yale University Press.

Laumann, E. O. and Knoke, D. (1987) *The Organizational State.* Madison, WI: University of Wisconsin Press.

Leeder, S. R. (1999) *Healthy Medicine: The Challenge Facing Australia's Health Services.* Sydney: Allen & Unwin.

Lewin, L (1991) *Self-interest and Public Interest in Western Politics.* New York: Oxford University Press.

Lindblom, C. E. (1959) The science of muddling through, *Public Administration Review,* 19: 78–88.

Lindblom, C. E. (1965) *The Intelligence of Democracy.* New York: Free Press.

Lindblom, C. E. (1979) Still muddling, not yet through, *Public Administration Review,* 39: 517–26.

Lindblom, C. E. and Woodhouse, E. J. (1993) *The Policy-making Process.* Englewood Cliffs, NJ: Prentice Hall.

Linder, S. H. and Peters, B. G. (1987) A design perspective on policy implementation: the fallacies of misplaced prescription, *Policy Studies Review*, 6: 459–75.

Lipsky, M. (1976) Towards a theory of street-level bureaucracy. In W. D. Hawley and M. Lipsky (eds) *Theoretical Perspectives on Urban Policy*. Englewood Cliffs, NJ: Prentice Hall.

Lipsky, M. (1980) *Street Level Bureaucracy*. New York: Russell Sage Foundation.

Lodge, M. (2003) Institutional choice and policy transfer: reforming British and German railway regulation, *Governance*, 16(2): 159–78.

Lukes, S. (1974) *Power: A Radical View*. London: Macmillan.

Lynn, L. E. (1999) A place at the table: policy analysis, its postpositive critics, and the future of practice, *Journal of Policy Analysis and Management*, 18(3): 411–25.

Majone, G. (1989) *Evidence, Argument and Persuasion in the Policy Process*. New Haven, CT; Yale University Press.

Majone, G. (2006) Agenda setting. In R. E. Goodin, M. Moran and M. Rein (eds) *The Oxford Handbook of Public Policy*. Oxford: Oxford University Press, pp. 228–50.

Maley, M. (2000) Conceptualising advisers' policy work: the distinctive policy roles of advisers on the Keating government, 1991–1996, *Australian Journal of Political Science*, 35: 449–70.

Maley, M. (2003) The growing role of ministerial advisers, *Canberra Bulletin of Public Administration*, no. 110 (Dec.): 1–4.

Maloney, W. A., Jordan, G. and McLaughlin, A. M. (1994) Interest groups and public policy: the insider/outsider model revisited, *Journal of Public Policy*, 14(1): 17–38.

March, J. G. and Olson, J. P. (1983) Organizing political life: what administrative reorganization tells us about government, *American Political Science Review*, 77(2): 281–96.

March, J. G. and Olsen, J. P. (1989) *Rediscovering Institutions*. New York: Free Press.

March, J. G. and Olsen, J. P. (2006) The logic of appropriateness. In R. E. Goodin, M. Moran and M. Rein (eds) *Oxford Handbook of Public Policy*. Oxford: Oxford University Press, pp. 689–708.

Marshall, J. and Peters, M. (eds) (1999) *Education Policy*. Aldershot: Edward Elgar.

May, P. J. (1992) Policy learning and failure, *Journal of Public Policy*, 12(4): 331–54.

McLean, I. (1987) *Public Choice: An Introduction*. Oxford: Basil Blackwell.

Meijerink, S. (2005) Understanding policy stability and change: the interplay of advocacy coalitions and epistemic communities, windows of opportunity, and Dutch coastal flooding policy 1945–2003, *Journal of European Public Policy*, 12(6): 1060–77.

Miller, H. T. and Demir, T. (2006) Policy communities. In F. Fischer, G. J.

Miller and M. Sidney (eds) *Handbook of Public Policy Analysis*. Boca Raton, FL: CRC Press, pp. 37–148.

Morgan, G. (1986) *Images of Organization*. Newbury Park, CA: Sage.

Morton, A. (2008) Heated reception for Garnaut, *The Age* (Melbourne), 10 July.

Mytelka, L. K. and Smith, K. (2002) Policy learning and innovation theory: an interactive and co-evolving process, *Research Policy*, 31(8/9): 1467–79.

Nelson, B. J. (1984) *Making an Issue of Child Abuse: Political Agenda Setting for Social Problems*. Chicago: University of Chicago Press.

Niskanen, W. A. (1973) *Bureaucracy and Representative Government*. Chicago: Aldine Atherton.

Noordegraaf, M. (2000a) *Attention! Work and Behavior of Public Managers amidst Ambiguity*. Delft: Eburon.

Noordegraaf, M. (2000b) Professional sense-makers: managerial competencies amidst ambiguity, *International Journal of Public Sector Management*, 13(4): 319–32.

Nutley, S. M., Walter, I and Davies, H. T. O. (2007) *Using Evidence: How Research Can Inform Public Services*. Bristol: Policy Press.

OECD/IEA (1992) *Climate Change Policy Initiatives*. Paris: OECD/IEA.

Osborne, B. and Gaebler, T. (1992) *Reinventing Government*. Reading, MA: Addison-Wesley.

Ostrom, V. and Sabetti, P. (1975) Theory of public policy. In S. S. Nagel (ed.) *Policy Studies in America and Elsewhere*. Lexington, MA: Lexington Books.

Outshoorn, J. (1991) Is this what we wanted? Positive action as issue peversion. In E. Meehan and S. Sevenhuijsen (eds) *Equality Politics and Gender*. London: Sage, pp. 104–21.

Pahl, J. (ed.) (1985) *Private Violence and Public Policy: The Needs of Battered Women and Responses of the Public Services*. London: Sage.

Painter, M. (1981) The coordination of urban policies: land use and transportation in North Sydney, 1970–75. In S. Encel and P. Wilenski (eds) *Decisions*. Melbourne: Longman Cheshire.

Painter, M. and Carey, B. (1979) *Politics between Departments*. St Lucia, University of Queensland Press.

Pal, L. A. (1995) Competing paradigms in policy discourse: the case of international human rights, *Policy Sciences*, 28(2): 185–207.

Palumbo, D. J. (ed.) (1987) *The Politics of Progam Evaluation*. Newbury Park, CA: Sage.

Parker, J. (2000) *Structuration*. Buckingham: Open University Press.

Parker, R. S. (1960) Policy and administration, *Public Administration* (Sydney), 19: 113–20.

Parsons, W. (1995) *Public Policy: An Introduction to the Theory and Practice of Policy Analysis*. Aldershot: Edward Elgar.

Pateman, C. (1983) Feminist critiques of the public/private dichotomy. In S. F. Benn and G. I. Gaus (eds) *Public and Private in Social Life*. London: Croom Helm, pp. 281–303.

Patton, C. V. and Sawicki, D. S. (1993) *Basic Methods of Policy Analysis and Planning*, 2nd edn. Englewood Cliffs, NJ: Prentice Hall.

Peters, B. G. and Pierre, J. (1998) Governance without governing, *Journal of Public Administration Research and Theory*, 8(2): 223–44.

Peters, B. G. and Pierre, J. (eds) (2006) *Handbook of Public Policy*. London: Sage.

Pierre, J. (ed.) (2000) *Debating Governance*. Oxford: Oxford University Press.

Pollitt, C. (2001) Joined-up government: a survey, *Policy Studies Review*, 1(1): 34–49.

Powell, W. W. and DiMaggio, P. J. (1991) *The New Institutionalism in Organizational Analysis*. Chicago, IL: University of Chicago Press.

Prasser, S. (2006) Aligning 'good policy' with 'good politics'. In H. K. Colebatch (ed.) *Beyond the Policy Cycle: The Policy Process in Australia*. Sydney: Allen & Unwin, pp. 266–92.

Pressman, J. and Wildavsky, A. (1973) *Implementation*. Berkeley: University of California Press.

Pressman, J. and Wildavsky, A. (1979) *Implementation*, 2nd edn. Berkeley: University of California Press.

Pressman, J. and Wildavsky, A. (1983) *Implementation*, 3rd edn. Berkeley: University of California Press.

Raab, J. and Kenis, P. (2007) Taking stock of policy networks: do they matter? In F. Fischer, G. J. Miller and M. S. Sidney (eds) *Handbook of Public Policy Analysis*. Boca Raton, FL: CRC Press, pp. 187–200.

Radin, B. (2000) *Beyond Machiavelli: Policy Analysis Comes of Age*. Washington, DC: Georgetown University Press.

Raedelli, C. (2003) *The Open Method of Coordination: A New Governance Architecture for the European Union?* Preliminary Report, Stockholm: Swedish Institute of Policy Studies.

Rhodes, R. A. W. (1997) *Understanding Governance*. Buckingham: Open University Press.

Rhodes, R. A. W. (2006) Policy networks. In R. E. Goodin, M. Moran and M. Rein (eds) *Oxford Handbook of Public Policy*. Oxford: Oxford University Press, pp. 425–47.

Richardson, J. (1984) The use of hospital and medical services in Australia: some policy issues. In M. Tatchell (ed.) *Perspectives on Health Policy*. Canberra: Australian National University Public Affairs Committee.

Richardson, J. J. (ed.) (1982) *Policy Styles in Western Europe*. London: Allen & Unwin.

Richardson, J. J. and Jordan, A. G. (1979) *Governing under Pressure*. Oxford: Martin Robertson.

Rochefort, D.A. and Cobb, R.W. (1994) *The Politics of Problem Definition: Shaping the Policy Agenda*. Lawrence: University Press of Kansas.

Roe, E. (1994) *Narrative Policy Analysis*. Durham, NC: Duke University Press.

Rose, N. (1999) *Powers of Freedom*. Cambridge: Cambridge University Press.

Rose, N. and Miller, P. (1992) Political power beyond the state: problematics of government, *British Journal of Sociology*, 43(2): 172–205.

Rosenau, J. N. and Czempiel, E-O. (eds) (1992) *Governance without Government: Order and Change in World Politics*. Cambridge: Cambridge University Press.

Rossi, P. H. and Freeman, H. (1993) *Evaluation: A Systematic Approach*. Newbury Park, CA: Sage.

Sabatier, P. A. (1986) Top-down and bottom-up approaches to implementation research: a critical analysis and suggested synthesis, *Journal of Public Policy*, 6: 21–48.

Sabatier, P. A. (ed.) (1999) *Theories of the Policy Process*. Boulder, CO: Westview Press.

Sabatier, P. A. and Jenkins-Smith, H. C. (1993) *Policy Change and Learning: An Advocacy Coalition Approach*. Boulder, CO: Westview Press.

Sabatier, P. A. and Mazmanian, D. (1979) The conditions of effective implementation: a guide to achieving policy objectives, *Policy Analysis*, 5: 481–504.

Sadonik, A.R. (2006) Qualitative research and public policy. In F. Fischer, G. J. Miller and M. Sidney (eds) *Handbook of Public Policy Analysis: Theory, Politics and Methods*. Boca Raton, FL: CRC Press, pp. 417–28.

Sanderson, I. (2002) Evaluation, policy learning and evidence-based policy making, *Public Administration*, 80(1): 1–22.

Schaffer, B. B. (1975) The problem of access to public services, *Development and Change*, 6: 3–11.

Schaffer, B. B. (1977) On the politics of policy, *Australian Journal of Politics and History*, 23: 146–55.

Schaffer, B. B. and Corbett, D. C. (1965) *Decisions*. Melbourne: Cheshire.

Schattschneider, E. E. (1960) *The Semisovereign People: A Realist's View of Democracy in America*. New York: Holt, Rinehart & Winston.

Schlager, E. (1995) Policy making and collective action: defining coalitions within the advocacy coalition framework, *Policy Sciences,* 28(3): 243–70.

Schmidt, M. R. (1993) Grout: alternative kinds of knowledge and why they are ignored, *Public Administration Review*, 53: 525–30.

Schön, D. and Rein, M. (1994) *Frame Reflection: Towards the Resolution of Intractable Policy Controversies*. New York: Basic Books.

Scott, W. R. (2001) *Institutions and Organization*, 2nd edn. Thousand Oaks, CA: Sage.

Scott, W. R. and Meyer, J. (1991) The organization of societal sectors: propositions and early evidence. In W. W. Powell and P. J. DiMaggio (eds) *The New Institutionalism in Organizational Analysis*. Chicago: University of Chicago Press, pp. 108–140.

Smith, G. and May, D. (1980) The artificial debate between rationalist and incremental models of decision-making, *Policy and Politics*, 8: 147–61.

Solesbury, W. (1976) The environmental agenda, *Public Administration*, 64: 379–97.

Stoker, G. (1998) Governance as theory: five propositions, *International Social Science Journal*, 50(155): 17–28.

Stone, D. A. (1988) *Policy Paradox and Political Reason*. Glenview, IL: Scott, Foresman.

Stone, D. A. (1989) Causal stories and the formation of policy agendas, *Political Science Quarterly*, 104(2): 281–300.

Stone, D. A. (1997) *Policy Paradox*. New York: Norton.

Stone, D. A. (1999) Learning lessons and transferring policy across time, space and disciplines, *Politics*, 19(1): 51–9.

Sylvester, R. (2008) Gordon Brown is being suffocated by a policy vacuum, *The Times*, 15 July.

Tao, J. L. (2006) Policy work at the local level in the United State whispers of rationality. In H. K. Colebatch (ed.) *The Work of Policy: An International Survey*. Lanham, MD, Lexington Books, pp. 181–98.

Taylor, S. (1984) *Making Bureaucracies Think*. Stanford, CA: Stanford University Press.

Tenbensel, T. (2004) Does more evidence lead to better policy? *Policy Studies*, 25(3): 189–207.

Tenbensel, T. (2006) Policy knowledge for policy work. In H. K. Colebatch (ed.) *The Work of Policy: An International Survey*. Lanham, MD, Lexington Books, pp. 199–215.

Throgmorton, J. A. (1991) The rhetorics of policy analysis, *Policy Sciences*, 24: 153–79.

Tinbergen, J. (1958) *The Design of Development*. Baltimore, MD: Johns Hopkins University Press.

Uhr, J. and Mackay, K. (1992) Trends in program evaluation: guest editors' introduction, *Australian Journal of Public Administration*, 51: 433–5.

Van Kersbergen, K. and Van Waarden, F. (2004) 'Governance' as a bridge between disciplines: cross-disciplinary inspiration regarding shifts in governance and problems of governability, accountability and legitimacy, *European Journal of Political Research*, 43(2): 43–71.

Van Waarden, F. (1992) Dimensions and types of policy networks, *European Journal of Political Research*, 21: 29–52.

Vedung, E. (2006) Evaluation research. In B. G. Peters and J. Pierre (eds) *Handbook of Public Policy*. London: Sage, pp. 397–416.

Vos, E. (1999) *Institutional Frameworks of Community Health and Safety Legislation*. Oxford: Hart.

Wallace, H. (ed.) (1986) *Policy-making in the European Community*, 2nd edn. Chichester: Wiley.

Walter, J. (1986) *The Minister's Minders: Personal Advisers in National Government*. Melbourne: Oxford University Press.

Walter, J. (2006) Ministers, minders and public servants: changing parameters of responsibility in Australia, *Australian Journal of Public Administration*, 65(3): 22–7.

Warren, M. (2008) Economist lays down the law on climate science, *The Australian,* 14 July.

Weible, C. M. and Sabatier, P. A. (2007) A guide to the advocacy coalition framework. In F. Fischer, G. J. Miller and M. S. Sidney (eds) *Handbook of Public Policy Analysis*. Boca Raton, FL: CRC Press, pp. 123–36.

Weick, K. E. (1979) *The Social Psychology of Organizing*, 2nd edn. Sydney: Allen & Unwin.

Weimer, D. and Vining, A. (2004) *Public Policy Analysis: Concepts and Practice*, 4th edn. Englewood Cliffs, NJ: Prentice Hall.

Weiss, C. H. (1982) Policy research in the context of diffuse decision-making. In *Policy Studies Review Annual,* Vol. 5, Beverly Hills, CA, Sage, pp. 19–36.

Weiss, C.H (1991) Policy research: data, ideas of arguments? In P. Wagner, C. Hirschon Weiss, B. Wittrock and H. Wollmann (eds) *Social Sciences and Modern States*. Cambridge: Cambridge University Press, pp. 307–32.

Wholey, J. (1981) Using evaluation to improve program performance. In R. A. Levine, M. A. Solomon, G-M. Hellstern and H. Wollman (eds) *Evaluation Research and Practice*. Beverly Hills, CA: Sage.

Wholey, J. and Hatry, J. S. (1992) The case for performance monitoring, *Public Administration Review*, 52(6): 604–10.

Wikipedia (2008) Policy. Available at http://en.wikipedia.org/wiki/Policy (accessed September 2008).

Wildavsky, A. (1979) *Speaking Truth to Power: The Art and Craft of Policy Analysis*. Boston: Little, Brown.

Wilson, W. (1887) The study of administration, *Political Science Quarterly*, 2: 197–222.

Yang, K. (2007) Quantitative methods for policy analysis. In F. Fischer, G. J. Miller and M. S. Sidney (eds) *Handbook of Public Policy Analysis*. Boca Raton, FL: CRC Press, pp. 349–68.

Yanow, D. (1996) *How Does a Policy Mean?* Washington, DC: Georgetown University Press.
Yanow, D. (2006) Qualitative-interpretive methods in policy research. In F. Fischer, G. J. Miller and M. Sidney, (eds) *Handbook of Public Policy Analysis: Theory, Politics and Methods.* Boca Raton, FL: CRC Press, pp. 405–16.

Index